CHANGE YOUR REALITY

CHANGE YOUR REALITY

Walt Adams

Change Your Reality
Copyright © 2020 by Walt Adams. All rights reserved.

No part of this publication may be reproduced, stored in a retrieval system or transmitted in any way by any means, electronic, mechanical, photocopy, recording or otherwise without the prior permission of the author except as provided by USA copyright law.

The opinions expressed by the author are not necessarily those of URLink Print and Media.

1603 Capitol Ave., Suite 310 Cheyenne, Wyoming USA 82001
1-888-980-6523 | admin@urlinkpublishing.com

URLink Print and Media is committed to excellence in the publishing industry.

Book design copyright © 2020 by URLink Print and Media. All rights reserved.

Published in the United States of America
ISBN 978-1-64753-204-8 (Paperback)
ISBN 978-1-64753-203-1 (Digital)
Non-Fiction
29.01.20

Contents

Chapter 1: Change 13
Chapter 2: How It Works 27
Chapter 3: Choose 39
Chapter 4: Tools 50
Chapter 5: The Ego And Consciousness 121
Chapter 6: Dreams 155
Chapter 7: Relationships. 162
Chapter 8: Manifesting Dis-Ease Physically 176
Chapter 9: The Rest Of The Story 194
Chapter 10: From omnipotence To Omnipotence. 229

Dedication

To you

Introduction

Most people believe, at least in part, that they create their own reality, but limit this to those aspects of life in which they have a considerable degree of interaction and control. The purpose of this book is to let you know that your realm of control extends far beyond your current concepts and even to the possible eventuality that YOU are Creator of your own reality and bring forth everything that affects you.

All is choice. The philosophical construct given here offers a potential for major change, and, as noted later in the book, no matter what you do, you can't do it wrong. Do what? Live your life.

The book is divided into three general sections. The first section (Chapters 1-3) covers the ideas behind how your reality works. The second section (Chapters 4-8) provides tools for changing it. The third section (Chapters 9 and 10) discusses the esoteric or non-physical aspects that pertain to living in our three dimensions.

The purpose of the book is to present a new paradigm of how things work on the planet. Examples, experiences and tools are presented to help you begin to accept your expanded ability to create your happiness.

For those of you who are familiar with Rhonda Byrne's book, *The Secret* and Pam Grout's book, *E-Squared*, it might appear that this is just another "visualization" book, but there is a significant difference. This book explains the mechanisms behind our behavior patterns (the why's) and provides tools (the how's) to change them.

Your current philosophy is the basis for the way you now live your life and an awareness of this will help you to understand why sometimes there is resistance towards some changes and enthusiasm towards others.

The information shared here can and will markedly change your concepts of your own power and its capability to produce a life filled with Joy, Happiness, Love and Peace. As in most things that are worthwhile, it will take work in retraining how you observe and react to your reality. As time passes and new behavior patterns are created, you will find yourself more comfortable with the success of your success, and the process can become a new and easy way to look at and create your own joy-filled life.

In regards to the information in this book, it is important that you set your mind before even starting to know that some things are going to feel right and some are not. Accept what you feel comfortable accepting and glide over the rest. You do not have to accept the whole philosophy to get benefits.

For some, the important part of the book is section 1, Chapters 1-3. This sets the concept in place and may be the only information you need. Section 3, the esoteric portion (Chapters 9 and 10) may also be of interest. As would be expected, the second section, (Chapters 4-8) is lengthy due to the large number of ideas that need to be covered. The purpose of the second section is to help in removing programming that no longer serves you.

In using the second section, it is worthwhile to read it in sequence as there is a development of philosophy and techniques that provide a natural learning progression to deal with problems.

In all of this, use your intuition to bring the change you desire. Think on this: You can't do it wrong.

Good journey.

Walt Adams

Chapter 1

CHANGE

This is the first word in the title and where we begin.

Change is the one thing in life that is fully guaranteed. There are those who live not paying taxes and there are those who say we never die and even those who say that physical immortality is possible. Maybe; maybe not. But in any case, change is ever-present in every aspect of our lives - sometimes in the smallest increments that we may never notice, like the changes in the mountains or the seas - sometimes in great increments, such as changing residences, or finding or losing a loved one. Change is always and forever. It can't be stopped no matter how hard we try. Having to constantly deal with change can be stressful, to say both the least - and the most. If we can learn to deal with change harmoniously and even learn to embrace it, we have a good beginning to achieving internal peace and harmony within ourselves and changing that which affects us.

Being conservative often means NOT wanting things to change. The resultant "closed" mind can significantly limit personal growth. An "open" mind allows for conservative philosophies but does not retreat from the possibilities that these ideas might be worth looking at in light of new information - potentially resulting in change.

"Locking" into a philosophical approach on any subject is done because it makes us feel "safe". Explanation of this mechanism is covered in Chapters 4 and 5. The idea is to embrace the possibility that what we "know" to be the truth just might not be totally correct any longer.

As we proceed through life, we generally feel that there are small portions where we can affect these changes and most of the rest is totally beyond our control. What we might hope for is an ability to fulfill this prayer attributed to Reinhold Niebuhr:

> "God grant me the serenity
> to accept the things I cannot change;
> courage to change the things I can;
> and wisdom to know the difference."

But there is a hitch here, and it is about degree. Most of us believe the degree we affect that which directly affects us may be large, but it is not 100 percent.

It is the intent of this book to show you that there is nothing in your life that you have not brought to yourself. It is brought to you through the Universal Law of Like Vibrations Attract (Chapter 2). This means that whatever you "put out there" is what you get. For most of us "what we put out there" is non-consciously created so we really don't know where or how our reality is created. Re-creating your reality is the essence of the book. Becoming aware is essential.

Is it possible to change the world through this personal work? The answer is an unqualified YES, but it, like any journey, starts with the first step and that is changing that which directly affects you. And <u>that</u> begins by changing yourself.

What is that first step?

A willingness to do the work to change.

Life has given each of us facts, experiences, knowledge and understanding that have continually changed as we have grown. So, too, has the manner in which we have used these assets. Adding perspective, discernment and insight often changes our view on any subject. Wisdom is putting our combined experiences into practice. Thus our wisdom has been as time-dependent as our thoughts, for as our experiences have accumulated, so has the basis from which we take action. In short, we have changed on a daily basis for our entire lives. The choice is to continue that change in directions we like, expressing thoughts, words and actions as in the past, or discerning those which don't serve us well and making desired changes.

Notice that what is described here is an intellectual approach to guide us on our journey. Due to the sequential nature of our human growth, most of the changes required to modify our vibration are of an emotional nature. This is further explained in Chapters 4 and 5.

We all live in a box. The "box" defines our "safe" space. What makes up this "box"? The bottom of the box is the foundation from which we make decisions. It consists of our species programming and the beliefs we have accepted as "truth". This "truth" takes many forms and colors both in how we process incoming information and how we act upon it. The walls are the experiences we have had that limit us because, as a whole, living "outside the box" is perceived by our programming to be dangerous. Experiences are the building blocks of the walls and fear is the mortar that holds the walls together. In this context, change is one of the most frightening, and thus the most limiting challenges to making the box bigger. By removing the limiting beliefs one reduces the fixed nature of the walls and allows the "box" to get bigger. Thus, totally removing all limiting beliefs eliminates the support for the roof, which doesn't fall in on you, but vanishes and allows you to soar.

Fear maintains the strength of the walls because "fear" is the mechanism used to keep us safe. Even unhappy situations are maintained inside this box because the thought of being able to deal with the unknown is perceived as much more dangerous than the situations with which we have learned to "live".

Most people hang on to their childhood experiences, beliefs and programming because this was the safest they have ever been. This is especially true of the very early years when mother was our everything and safe - oh so safe!

The function of this book is to help you find those systems that continue to limit you and eliminate them, thus enlarging your "box" and perhaps releasing you to fly free for the fist time in your life.

Most of us have reduced the allowable events in our lives because of the "hurtful" things that have happened both physically and emotionally. Thus the sense of adventure in us has been reduced to near zero. Can you remember a time when you wanted to be adventuresome? Go there again and bring it forward. Carry that with you through this work and know that the wondrous child within still exists.

Here are the keys to the beginning of this process.
The first requirement in bringing about change is:

Desire.

Usually the desire for change comes from a situation that we do or do not like. For purposes of this work, we shall discuss those we do not like, for if you like something, why would you want to change it?

This desire for change comes from situations that are generally unpleasant and therefore you want to change them. It can also come from a situation which is not particularly unpleasant, but you desire to change it simply because the alternative is more appealing. In either case, there is incentive for change, and at some point that intensity may become great enough to warrant, even demand, change. We will go into these limitations and how to remove them from our vibration in the second section.

The second requirement for change is:

> Persistence.

As with any plant or animal that grows in this three-dimensional universe, everything takes time. If you give up before the work bears visible fruit, it won't continue by itself, primarily because your giving up creates the vibration of "failure" which guarantees nothing will happen. "This doesn't work" creates a reality in which whatever it is will indeed not work. Richard Bach, in his book *Illusions* puts it well:

> "Argue for your limitations and sure enough, they're yours"

So, make the work a habit.
The third requirement is:

> Awareness

Most of us go through life on automatic, aware of little more than that something just happened. What is required as a significant part of this work is remaining in the present, the eternal NOW. This needs to be done in order to see that something is or is not as you would like it, and to be aware of your own re-actions. This awareness will allow you to make and recognize changes in the present and perhaps create the possibility that when not-so stressful events do occur, they will get your attention. This is not unlike "heading them off at the pass" before a problem becomes larger.

There is another "requirement" which is not really a requirement, but is very helpful in doing this work. It is:

Patience

Patience is not a natural part of the human condition. It has to be learned. Fast food; "I want what I want and I want it NOW"; "I don't see anything happening" and "It's taking too long" won't get you where you want to go any more quickly, it will only add a degree of frustration which will hinder your work. This attribute is probably one of the hardest to conquer, for it flows over into most everything we do. Remember it took you years to physically grow up and accumulate the programming you now have. Consequently, it will take time to reprogram.

Once in a while it will be worth looking back over the time you have worked (weeks, months, years) to see that there has indeed been significant progress.

The greatest part of the learning in regard to patience is patience with yourself and the natural way your systems work.

In pursuing this work there is a thought to keep in mind:

> You can only blame your parents and
>   circumstances for your programming
>   for so long.
>
> It is YOU who perpetuates it.

In short, it is all choice - yours.

The resistance to changing our paradigms is rooted in our experiences. These set the baseline filters from which we allow changes to occur. We are all heavily invested in our own truth and will often defend it to the death. While this may seem irrational, it is a necessary part of our creating a "safe" environment in which to live - our "box".

Many childhood behavior patterns are hugely inclusive and viewed from a "black or white" absoluteness due to the lack of physiological and psychological development. They can remain cornerstones of our world view for our entire lives. Keeping this in mind may help you to be more open to change.

Here are some beliefs that can overlay your entire psyche:

I have no value.
I am useless.
I am unworthy.
I am not deserving.
There is always a price to pay (strings) for any gift.
I am afraid of everything.
Everything is either black or white. (absolute thinking)
I do not trust myself.
The truth is not a good thing.
Fearing the unknown.
I am a bad (evil?) person.
I am stubborn.
I am powerless.
I am stupid.
I am a failure.

Your philosophy is strictly yours. It is the starting point for change. Someone can tell you something as much as they want, but if it doesn't fit into your philosophy (which may include the attitude towards new information), then it will automatically be rejected. Until you have personally had experiences to validate a new paradigm, that paradigm will always be doubted. So this too is a requirement of this work and that is to look for experiences that either do or do not validate the new ideas.

As you get further into the changes, you will find that there will be pivotal experiences that change your outlook significantly from "well, I don't know", to "maybe", to "yes, I totally believe that now." You have had such experiences already as part of the formation of your current philosophy. This is simply the way we work.

So here I would like to share such an experience that led me from "perhaps" to "I now believe this is true". It is in regards to what I share in Chapter 2, concerning "Like Vibrations Attract".

When I first moved to New York City I had to have a vehicle to pick up and deliver materials for my work, which was construction. Every week I got at least one ticket and sometimes two. At $50 a ticket at the time, this really frosted my butt. I would grumble and moan and pay the fines and it just continued no matter how careful I was. This went on for 7 months. A good sample, no?

One day I was working on the 19th floor of a building. I had parked 2 blocks away at a meter and plunked in my quarters. When I got to the apartment, there were no clocks working because it was under renovation, so I guessed about the right time, went back to the car to put in more quarters, got the ticket off the windshield, grumbled accordingly and put it on the front seat. I then moved the car to another parking meter across the street from the building where I was working. I carefully noted the time and returned to the apartment where this time, I had a clock working. At approximately 5 minutes before the allotted time, I left the apartment and went to the elevator, pushed the button and waited. And waited. I was just about to run down the stairs when I heard the ding and got on. It was a local. As we inched down the 19 floors my anxiety grew in proportion, but hey, I was really close. Got to the car and there was another ticket on the windshield. No meter maid in sight. The time was right and the meter expired. I lost it. The

Change Your Reality

day was ruined. TWO tickets in one day. TWO ! I railed and ranted at the Universe and the world in general, said many nasty words and finally screamed to the skies (silently, but in New York City who would have noticed) "OK. OK!! O K !!! I WILL address it, damnit I will address it." Plunked in more quarters with great gusto, went back up to the apartment, finished the day and went home.

And I "addressed" it.

Using techniques I will share with you in the second section, I found that I had a real problem with authority. Police, firemen, meter maids, lines on parking lots, anything that inclined to control me in any way. I hated and feared this control and, simply put, the vibration was so powerful that I attracted the very nature of the vibration to myself almost every day! For me, and most others, fear is the most powerful creative energy we express, for it is driven by survival and is highly emotionally charged. This fear had to be eliminated to change the situation. I brought perspective to the situation and changed my attitude. I couldn't fake it. I really had to change my attitude. Well I did, because for the next seven months I didn't receive a single ticket. I even got to the point where I pushed the envelope and still didn't get one.

This set of events brought the concept home for me. The issue was probabilities. The probabilities of not having a parking ticket for seven months in New York City, after having one or two a week for the same period of time is infinitesimal. Something had to have happened to effect a change. Being trained as an engineer, the only thing that changed was my attitude (vibration) - and it did indeed change the situation instantaneously.

Pivotal points are the cornerstone of changes in philosophy. Only YOU can have them.

The pivotal points need not be as dramatic as this, for they can be any event that moves you from "perhaps-believing" to "knowing" and they can occur in a second, and change your life forever!

There is a natural aspect of our humanity that plays a major part in your reality and cannot be ignored. It is the genetically driven need to survive. This will appear in many guises in the formation of your current behavior patterns and dealing with this and changing it is an integral part of the tools shared in section 2. There is a built-in resistance to change. It is deeply seated in the experience of our species based on those who went out on their own, without thinking, and got eaten. Those who were more cautious were more likely to survive. This aspect of our beingness - fear - is the only real limit we have to being totally happy. We will again go into dealing with this extensively as we look into the obvious and not-so obvious triggers of fear in section 2.

In Bruce Lipton's *The Biology of Belief*, it is noted that the conscious mind is capable of processing about 40 bits of environmentally-stimulated events per second, while in that same period of time the non-conscious mind is processing 20,000,000 bits. What this five-hundred-thousand to one ratio says very clearly is:

> "Trying to control your non-conscious with your conscious mind, without it being in synergy, is virtually impossible."

If fears run your show, as it does in part for most people, you have to bring some pretty big tools to the game to have any chance of making progress. Well the thrust of this book is to bring the "pretty big tools" to accomplish those very changes and achieve that synergy. As this occurs, you will notice that there will be fewer reaction-causing triggers and it will become easier to "go with the flow".

Whereas the reptilian brain is the manifesting agent for our fears, our consciousness is the part of us that decides what is safe or not from its limited experiences. We need to modify our "software" to update those criteria.

In this book we shall use the term non-conscious to refer to all that goes on in the brain which is not conscious, i.e., that of which you are not aware. This differs from the standard psychoanalytical terms relating to consciousness for a reason. The reason being that the non-conscious (in my terms) includes everything from all experiences in both physical and non-physical realms and internal interactions. The reason for this will become obvious in Chapter 2.

Changing of the non-consciousness is NOT a battle; it is a progression into synergism with your self. The idea is that your conscious and non-conscious are capable of a wondrous, joyous harmony. In some esoteric circles "enlightenment" is considered the achieving of total synergy between the conscious and non-conscious parts of our being.

From even before being born, the non-consciousness is processing environmental data. As the natural capabilities of the brain develop, the synapses begin to connect in associative ways. This process continues for as long as you live.

There is one more point worth making before we get to the core of the book. It is this:

Perfection is in the eye of the beholder.

There are two definitions of perfection. The first is the human concept that can be represented by the following example:

Take a perfectly flat, smooth piece of paper or velum. Take a very fine pointed ink pen. Take a perfectly straight edged ruler. Draw a straight line using the ruler and pen on the paper. Remove the pen and ruler and look at the line. "Perfect!!" Right?

Wrong!

How? Look at the line through a microscope and it will look like a winding path on Mount Everest. Look at it through an electron microscope and there won't be any line at all! It is a matter of resolution as to how "perfect" it is. This is true for every human endeavor, including science. Each "proof" is only a little less inaccurate than the one before.

The second is the cosmic concept of perfection and that is:

>What is <u>IS</u> Perfect.
>Just the way it is.
>Now.

This is the definition used throughout the book when the word "perfect" is used.

As children, our concept of "perfection" is based on what we see and how we process this information within our brains. The brain of a child is incapable of bringing discernment to some situations because it has not yet developed to an extent whereby the synapsis to completely asses a situation are available. Further, the knowledge-base is limited by experience. These come with the natural process of growing up. Yet during these formative years we "lock in" many of the beliefs that color our perception throughout our lives. As an example, we might perceive that we are a "failure" at something or all things. With the greater perspective that you can't do it wrong (it is all part of growing up), this makes the thought that one is a "failure" completely erroneous.

Failure, as success, is in the eyes of the beholder

I would like to share a quote from Ken Carey's book *Starseed, The Third Millennium:*

"To live spontaneously, instinctually. To simply be. To say the right words without thinking them out ahead of time. To experience the purity of a mind uncluttered by troublesome and misplaced responsibility. To know exactly the right gesture, the right behavior, the creative responses for each and every situation. Such are the birthrights of each and every human being."

Question: How much proof do you need to know this system works?

Answer: However much you need. It is totally personal.

In any undertaking there are moments of discouragement. To allow for these as being an integral part of this project, it can help to sometimes put it all aside for a while. In all of nature, growth is cyclical. There are times of activity (day for plants) and rest (night). There are times of forward movement and times of sliding back. It is all natural and part of our inherited humanness. Knowing that the overall view is one of forward movement and progress is a good thought to keep in mind. In this regard there is a saying my brother shared with me which is totally appropriate. It is this:

> When you're up to your ass in alligators, it's
> really hard to remember your goal was to
> empty the swamp.

And one final thought in this chapter. When looking at a large job, it is easy to be overwhelmed by the amount of work that appears to have to be accomplished. Remember, you are reprogramming years and perhaps eons of experience. This will indeed take time. The only way to approach this task is to divide the work into little parts and take one day and one step at a time.

You are doing the best you can under the pressures of programming. Be kind to yourself.

A word of encouragement:

It will take very little change to convince you that you really do have the ability to significantly re-create your life. You need but be aware of what is going on around you. At the same time patience is necessary because all the situations in which you find yourself have the inertia that goes along with living in the physical. This is partially because you have interactions with all those around you and there will be additional things to think about as you move along. Know that just reading this material begins the process and that while much of what you read you may not totally remember, your non-conscious mind remembers it all and will lead you back here when appropriate. The journey into change is well worth the price of doing the work.

It is again worthwhile for you to remember as you move along in the process that the ego and programming are not enemies, they simply are aspects of yourself you are going to change.

With this all behind us, let's move into the realm of actually changing our reality.

Chapter 2

HOW IT WORKS

Like Vibrations Attract

This is how your reality is created.

"Like Vibrations Attract" is the core of how things work in the physical and non-physical Universe. There are no exceptions. While that statement seems to be a bit dramatic and all-inclusive, it is, nonetheless, true, as you will come to discover for yourself.

Every major teacher of every religion has shared the concept of "Like Vibrations Attract" in words of their language and time. They all knew how simple the law of attraction operates and how we bring on our own circumstances and fates. In this book we are simply bringing forward their knowledge into a current time, space and language. The mysteries and secrets of the past are no longer hidden. They are simple, present and available in this moment.

The first question that needs to be asked is what is a "vibration". We all have heard or used "someone has good vibes", but what does that mean? A vibration can best be described as a frequency, but it is not the same as the term used to describe the waveforms which include everything from the movement of earthquakes to sound to light to radio frequencies to the speed of a computer chip and on up the ladder of "cycles per second" with which we are familiar.

So, what is it? Good question. Although you know what we mean when we say "vibrations" in this context, science has no description of exactly what it is. The concept of "like vibrations attract" has the same effect as the attraction of a magnet for iron, yet it includes two people coming together in a relationship, drawing "accidents" to ourselves and belonging to a stamp club because those are people who are of "like mind" in their personal pursuits. It has been suggested that the "vibration" of which we speak is of a "quantum" nature (multidimensional), and therefore not totally physical. This might explain the difficulty in describing it.

The complexities of Quantum Entanglement generally explain how everything is connected. Science says that everything is energy in different forms, some of which are not yet explainable. This connectedness is the bridge between the physical and non-physical realities. Thought has a measureable vibrational component that interacts with the more "physical" world around us. This is why and how we can affect physical change. In addition, in the "vibrational world", distance is meaningless.

In the following chapters we shall give many examples of the manifestation of this concept and it is strongly suspected that by the end of the book, you will easily see the workings of the concept both outside and within your own personal reality.

Our significant programming essentially begins as the baby develops in the womb. We take in the stimuli of our environment and process it through the capabilities at our disposal. This amounts to a very limited world view that results in all-inclusive reactions that are programmed to keep us "safe".

Again, in Bruce Lipton's book *The Biology of Belief*, an in-depth exploration of this is covered.

Change Your Reality

As we grow, the human brain expands to allow for new interpretations and programmatic responses to the environment. As we progress through the advent of puberty and whatever learnings we experience into adulthood, we remain tied to our early programming, much of which turns out to be limiting. The human animal is the only one that will continue to try a "successful" action even if it has not worked a thousand times after the first "success". That's just the way it is.

For many of you one of the first questions might be: "If Like Vibrations Attract, then what is my vibration and what am I creating?"

You have created EVERYTHING that is in and <u>affecting</u> you in your reality now. You need only look around your own life and you will see a perfect reflection of your vibration.

Again for many of you this is a bit hard to take, for why would you bring into your reality something that you consciously do NOT want there?

The key, of course, is the word "consciously". If you go into the physiology of the human animal it will become clear that very little of what we do is conscious (remember Bruce Lipton's ratio of 40 to 20,000,000 bits in the previous chapter?). By our very nature, we set behavior patterns into action to do almost everything. It, whatever "it" is, becomes an automatic response to initiating instructions, such as walking, driving, eating, arguing and the like. There are few exceptions. All of these events, while triggered by a conscious (maybe) starting point, are controlled by the non-conscious.

NOTE: Remember, in this book "non-conscious" means all that is not of the conscious mind.

Here is an example to assist in understanding how our habits work:

When you commute to work and walk or drive the same way every day, you set up an automatic set of patterns wherein you turn left or right at specific corners to get you where you want to go. You set these actions in your non-conscious and trigger the beginning of the playback as you leave home and head out for the day. (It takes approximately two weeks to create new behavior patterns.) One day you decide to take a small detour to do something on the way to work and off you go. You sail past the turn to your alternate destination and don't realize it until you've passed the turn. A great deal of your life is run by setting your beginning point in some action (the 40 bit part) and letting your non-consciousness (the 20,000,000 bit part) do the rest. These patterns become an integral part of your living. It is because of this that a single stimulus to want to change something doesn't make the old pattern just go away. There needs to be reprogramming. This takes time and effort, requiring conscious awareness and patience.

Especially patience.

And here is one of the most important points to be made in this work. We will make it again in Chapter 4. It is in regard to judgment of your self.

> You have always done the best you can with what you have.
> What you "have" is "stuff"
> (programming).
> Everyone's got "stuff".

"Coming down" on yourself for just having made a wrong turn (decision) only feeds a poor self-image. Simply recognizing the error and saying next time I shall do better, and letting the judgment go, is the most appropriate and powerful response.

Change Your Reality

The event can also be a reminder that being aware in the moment is the key to change.

The greatest imperative in human life is safety. It overshadows every action we take. In Maslow's *Hierarchy of Needs*, the pyramid of consciousness has at the bottom, basic survival actions. At the top is self-actualization. No matter where you are at any one time on this pyramid, if some survival situation occurs (having to go to the bathroom real bad) as perceived by your programming, you will instantaneously revert to the bottom and deal with it. Safety is the trigger and perceived need is the driving energy.

As little children we are open to most anything. Outside of the natural triggers (starving and stuff like that), our experience shows us that something is unsafe. Perhaps triggering mother's or father's anger, putting your hand on something hot, etc. In time, through "hurtful" events, those things we will allow narrows considerably and we take fewer chances because we inherently feel the world is unsafe and perhaps "out to get us". Gated communities and narrow thinking are the natural fallout of life as we have experienced it. Fear is always the driving force and ignorance the cause. Fear is the ONLY limit we have to opening the door to creating anything we might like.

Fear is the most powerful creative energy we have. Love is more powerful, but most of us are somewhat limited in our ability to be and express it.

The child holds the greatest potential opportunity in our lives to experience joy and bliss because it is the simple joy of living coming from the heart. It is not yet tainted by "real" world experiences and programming. It has been said that entry into heaven is easiest for the innocent child.

Unfortunately, "Like Vibrations Attract" says very clearly that that which we fear we will attract to us, and that is exactly the way it works.

Later on we will discuss the nature of some of these fears and share tools to eliminate them, but for now let us continue to discuss the nature of the "vibration" which is creating your current reality.

The vibration is made of five general components. They are:

1. The genetic makeup that you inherited from your parents (their parents, your species, etc.).
2. The sum total of effects of all the events/circumstances of this life.
3. The significant events carried over from other lives, including benign (piano playing), exhilarating (exceeding joy) and painful (starving to death).
4. The energy of the totality of your Beingness - that part of you that is the singularity within the All. Some call this the "Higher Self" and/or the "Soul".
5. The Universal Oneness, The Whole.

Each level of vibration is nosier than the previous. As in Maslow's *"Hierarchy of Needs"*, when the nosier aspect of the vibrations is activated, the person will go to that level to deal with the stimulus. The higher levels of our vibration still exist underneath, but are overshadowed by the noise. Quieting this "noise" is the goal in many meditation practices. Eventually, with practice, you can be functioning from a high level most of the time without the need for "going into meditation".

The first level, your genetics, is the source of the need for safety. Its manifestation is through experiences that have proven dangerous and therefore a fear of repeating them is present. The "holder" and "processor" of fear-based responses is the reptilian brain, the first "brain" to be developed in the evolving human. The operational component of these fears is the consciousness, whose job it is to keep you safe. It does this by taking what it knows from experience to be dangerous and projecting it into the future. If it perceives that this new event is "dangerous", it makes itself known through fear.

Genetics also bring the instinctual fears and automatic responses that have developed over the history of human evolvement. They contain natural fears such as those of being abandoned, starving and change. Regarding change, if you think about it, it appears that change is a natural-based fear as well. As an example, watch a usually precocious young child hide behind its parent's leg when a stranger walks in the room, or notice your own anxiety about any major change. It is all based on safety. Change has a fear factor based on natural selection, where those who changed too quickly got eaten by lions, tigers and bears. For humans, change must be made in small steps to stay below the radar of an instinctually-triggered fear response.

Fear is the most powerful creational energy we have because it is so emotionally intense (noisy).

It is very important to note that fear is not the only energy that creates this reality by a long shot. It is only the most energetic. The entire idea of recreating your reality is based on the joy of having your desires manifest. Again, we are addressing that which we wish to change, not the joy and happiness we have as part of our expression at this time.

The second most powerful creational aspect of our vibration is this-life experiences. Experiences create new experiences on top of the old, but seldom, unless specifically addressed, do the fear aspects of experiences go away naturally. This is because they bring forth safety responses from the genetic level.

The human being has a huge brain capacity and has never developed a natural response to eliminate no-longer-functional fear responses. This tends to give humans a greater awareness of potential dangers and therefore more safety responses. As a direct consequence, the human will continue to try any response that worked once for a problem, long after it is obvious that it doesn't work any more. Other animals with more limited brain capacity tend to learn more quickly that something no longer works.

Therapy in its many forms can help us move out of the fear base. The approaches shared here, and in many books, can easily be thought of as a therapy in those terms. The work is to disconnect or redirect the synapses that are limiting or damaging through disuse and replace them with more harmonious connections through conscious directions and actions.

The non-conscious sees everything and chooses, based on experience, which, what and how to incorporate into our operating system that which it considers appropriate. Thus everything contributes to your vibration in some manner, be it small or large.

The third part of your vibration is from other lives. This information is transmitted to your present life through a mechanism called cellular memory. It is the DNA in all 37 trillion of your cells that remembers all your history. The process is similar to putting rum on a cake after it has been baked and having it permeate the whole cake. As the seed of consciousness is brought forth into the baby, it contains memories from previous experiences. The memories are of two general types. Those that come from repetitious patterns, (playing the piano, living in Paris, loving animals, the mountains, etc.) and, more importantly for us here, those that are highly emotionally charged. These latter emotions come from intense experiences such as drowning, being tortured, taking vows, intensely loving another person and anything you can imagine. There may also be hereditary characteristics such as predisposition to food, alcohol and philanthropy.

In general these "other life" experiences will manifest through a similar tendency in this life and only after you have dealt with these this-life aspects, noting that the behavior you wish to change still exists, might you find it worthwhile to investigate other lives to seek the source. Tools in Chapters 4 and 9 offer methodologies for looking into other lives.

The fourth level from which we create our vibration is what some call our "Higher Self/soul energy ". It can have many names but it is that aspect of our own consciousness that is always in tune with the Cosmic All. This is not someone else. This is YOU and this aspect of ourselves is always present. It has a relatively high vibration which most of the time is overshadowed by the coarser (noisier) vibrational levels of numbers 1, 2 and 3 above.

The fifth level is the Universal Oneness, (God or whatever term is comfortable for you). This level is present in us all, but is seldom experienced because of all the other "noise" that masks It's presence.

The point of consciousness that is you in the physical has all of this as a part of its being. Everyone is unique and therefore each person's mix of these is dependent on your focus at any moment in time.

Creative thought creates new vibrations that add to the total vibration you express every moment of your waking and sleeping lives.

The question now becomes; "So what do I do with all this information? It sounds like we are getting very complicated. Where do we go from here?"

Where we go is to Chapter 3. Choices. But before we do that, there are some other things worth including in your knowledge base. So bear with us.

Choices set in motion the changes which will naturally occur wherein all the seeming limitations to our happiness will become just that - seeming. And then vanishing. This action will have a most interesting effect on your reality, for in order to remove the limitations to your happiness, the Energy of the Universe MUST bring forth circumstances, situations, events, tools and whatever else is needed to remove ALL blockages to your happiness. How does it do this?

There is a paradox concerning what the Universe is and how it operates. It is this:

1. The Universe is 100% impersonal.
2. The Universe is 100% personal.

The Universe can be likened to a giant computer that requires instructions. It is impersonal in this regard. The "instructions" we give to the universal computer in order to create our reality is our "vibration". If your "vibration" is conscious, you will have a clear creation of what that is. If it is unclear, your reality will be wishy-washy. For most of us, when asked what we want, we really don't know. It's a little bit of this and a little bit of that, and that's what we get.

The universal computer has no choice but to bring your vibrational instruction into your reality. Interesting thought, isn't it? It really works this way. You will come to find this "truth" through your own investigations.

What is the "personal" aspect of the Universe? Here it will require a stretch for some, but at least be open to the ideas. The "personal" aspects of your reality are the "rest of you". This is you. Your higher self, your Soul. You also have angels and guardians that are present as well. There are many books that cover the function of these energies.

Note: It should be pointed out here that the belief in such "helpers" and esoterica mentioned later in the book do NOT have to become a part of your philosophical construct for the concepts and tools for changing your reality to work. Certainly the greatest percentage of programming that may warrant change is a result of the very physical stages of 1 and 2, and the emphasis of this book is heavily on dealing with stimuli generated from these levels.

Change Your Reality

There is one final and pivotal point to ponder:

You do not directly create your reality. You create your vibration, which, through the mechanism of the energy of the Universe, creates your reality.

You are the writer and director of your play as well as the player, but not the producer. The production is mounted by the Universe.

Another point:

> The pleasure center is in the brain.
> The joy center is in the heart.

One more story: I am driving down Interstate 81 and my passenger is in a bad mood. The mood begins to affect me and I become more agitated as we continue. I decide to stop for something to eat and take a break at a McDonalds. I order an Oreo McFlurry. When I get it, I don't see any Oreo bits so I ask the server to add some to which she says we aren't allowed to add two condiments, but she does and I take it only to find out that she made an M&M McFlurry, not an Oreo McFlurry. The point? My agitation got me the "chaos" of the wrong dessert. There are many stories like this. Check your own. When you are upset, your vibration will create chaos. It pays to be centered and calm. The greater the upsettedness, the greater the chaos!

And now to one of the most important concepts of this work. The questions is:

A question almost everyone asks at some time in their life is:

> Who am I?

The answer for everyone is:

You are the Love of the Universe (God) manifest as a point of consciousness in the present.
Everything else is what you do.

Now on to the work.

Chapter 3

CHOOSE

Life, death, responsibilities, family relationships, children, having to work, eating, sleeping, and everything else are all components that we have in our lives. We are "burdened" by the endless things that we "have" to do in this reality and situations and circumstances in which we find ourselves.

Perhaps some lend themselves to choice, but many do not - or so it appears. Take each of those things listed above and look at whether there is an alternative. Of course there is. BUT your choice in each matter is dependent on many personal factors. AND in each of the situations listed above, and the rest of what is in your life, you have indeed taken part in deciding to do whatever it is you are now doing. Many of those choices were non-consciously made and you are living the results. Many of these situations do not lend themselves easily to change, but most do to some degree.

So, what now? How do I change all this to make my life something I actually want to continue?

Choose consciously.

What do I choose and to whom, and to what do I make the choices?

In the previous chapter, you were introduced to the concept of the impersonal universe, the "computer" that needs instructions to make things happen. That is where you direct your "choices".

Choice is usually non-consciously generated from experiential-based programming, desires or dreams. Once in a while it is made from conscious awareness. It is preferable to come from the latter.

How do you direct your choices so that they are brought to pass?

Through the conscious verbal (out loud) statement of what it is you want with the express <u>intention</u> of "instructing the Universe".

What choices do I make, especially considering the "mess" in which I currently find myself?

Let us give you an example of a choice.

Following this "choice", we will explain why it works.

The initial "instruction":

Universe, God, the IS (whatever constitutes the ultimate power of the Universal oneness to you)

I Choose to be happy.
Make it so!

Work to <u>feel</u> that what you just did has the power to make it happen.

BECAUSE IT DOES!

To reinforce this action, <u>start</u> off every day by saying:
"I Choose to Be Happy"
It's that simple.

Later we will add other possibilities of choice and why they may be right for you, but that is what you do. Every day - Choose to BE Happy - maybe even several times. With this statement and all visualizing statements it is imperative to put in the greatest feelings of joy and energy and really FEEL the happiness from today's events. It is also necessary that you believe that "happiness" is possible for you in your reality. At the end of each day, do a review and ask yourself if you had a happy day. Review the specific items that brought forth a feeling of happiness. In time, the number of days that qualify will increase. This review brings to your conscious mind what you are working to accomplish and keeps it fresh. In doing this you automatically raise your vibration.

The following is the basis of why "I Choose to Be Happy" works.

1. Like Vibrations Attract is the operating modality for the Universe, both physical and non-physical. You "magnetize" everything to you through this mechanism.
2. Waking consciousness is the most powerful vibrational aspect of your being.
3. The Universe is a huge AUTOMATIC "computer" that responds to instructions.
4. The Universe does not respond to begging It needs to be INSTRUCTED what to do.
5. You are the captain (creator) of your reality and therefore the director, the programmer. You are acknowledging this by this statement.
6. Your reality is all about you. Not anyone else. Others are involved but they are there because you attracted them to you as they did you to them.
7. We all have chosen a commonality for our work, it is called planet Earth. It is our stage.

8. Your reality consists primarily of those things that affect you. External news events are just that - external - and may have an effect on your vibration but you will almost never affect them in your daily creation nor will they affect you directly.
9. The word "I" tells the Universe that you are present and aware as an individualized consciousness.
10. The word "Choose" tells the Universe that you are capable, ready, willing and able to assume responsibility for creating your reality and are establishing your all-important <u>intent</u>.
11. The words "to Be" means "exist in" as opposed to "do". "Doing" happiness would be making up things to do just to be happy. "Being" happy allows that you can be totally content and at peace doing anything - or nothing. Are you are ready to exist in a state of Happiness?

It is important to understand that "existing in a state of happiness" is of a general nature. It is best to leave it in this context rather than be specific for four reasons:

1. The Universe KNOWS what makes you happy! It is all encompassing and is aware of every aspect of every vibration at all times and takes all of this into account in responding to your "instruction". There are too many factors for you to put it all together since you don't have either the capability or the database.
2. You don't know what makes you happy. Although you think you know what "happiness" is, you probably don't, because of the complex interactions of the myriad of factors that create that condition within you at any one moment.

Change Your Reality

3. Your happiness is time dependent. What made you happy this morning is different from what will make you happy now, or a year from now.
4. If you are specific, you limit your happiness by limiting the Universe as to how it may respond to your instruction.

For those of you who are familiar with *The Secret* by Rhonda Byrne, there may seem to be a contradiction between her - "be specific" - recommendations and the - "keep it general" - concept recommended here. There isn't. It is not one or the other, it is a combination of both put together by you with the perspective of how it works and what you want. For example: You want a Porsche. Well, you want a specific car. Period. Well, again, maybe not. What you want is the "Perfect" car for you. Your vibration is so strong towards Porsche that this will dominate whether you say Porsche or not. But then the "Perfect" car for you might actually be something different because there are factors (comfort, handling, image, design, etc.) that you wouldn't really know whether you did or didn't like until you actually had one. The Universe KNOWS what will be "Perfect" for you on all levels, so seeing yourself driving the "Perfect" car may or may not have you ending up with a Porsche. "Like vibrations attract" brings to you the Perfect manifestation of that vibration.

Generality does not preclude specificity.

You would probably end up with the Porsche anyway. However,
Here is a worthwhile point to keep in mind:

> The clearer the instruction,
> The greater the probability of
> getting what you want.
> More quickly.

The clarity of the instruction is measured by the LACK of competing vibrational components. An example would be where you want your business to succeed, but non-consciously there is also the element that part of you doesn't want to be in business at all. This could be because of experiences of trouble with clients, manufacturers, suppliers or wanting to be somewhere else or any number of other reasons. In addition you may think, at some level, that you don't deserve unbridled success or are afraid of success or failure. On and on the reasons may go.

A concept to help understand how the Universe operates is the idea of an "and" gate and an "or" gate as used in electronics. Think of an electrical battery and a light bulb with many switches in between. If they are hooked up in series it would require every switch to be closed to have the light go on. This is an "and" gate. This switch "and" the next "and" the next etc. have to be closed to get the light to light.

If all the switches are hooked up in parallel, then any switch closing will turn on the light. This switch "or" that switch "or" that switch, etc.....

For us, the way the Universe operates is an "and" gate. All the programming that limits our achieving our freedom must be closed, one item at a time. Seems daunting, doesn't it? Not necessarily. Some limitations have only a single "switch". The complexity of any one problem is directly related to the number of items that went to create the situation.

For the "clarity" we desire for the Universe to respond to our instructions, it is desirable to have the number of "and" gates reduced. This we do through the processes of reprogramming.

In short: The will of the Universe is the same as yours. Only YOU stand in the way of your happiness.

As far as interpersonal relationships go, your desire may, to a large extent, be based on what went wrong before, or some programmatic predisposition. Chances are REALLY good that you don't know what a "Perfect" relationship would be. Here generality is by far the better choice. Leave it to the Universe.

OK - so what IS happiness for you? If you are like most people, happiness is Love, Peace, Contentment, Harmony, a feeling of well-being, physical /emotional /mental/spiritual wellness, awareness and a feeling of joy towards yourself and life as a whole, and having fun.

Happiness is joy in the moment and requires an awareness of your self in the present. Joy is a feeling, an emotion. It needs to be recognized and acknowledged in order to create an atmosphere of happiness. Joy is different from other emotions in that it tends to be a quick spike and then, just as quickly, fades. Recognition requires awareness, and from this, actions or behavior patterns which create joy and happiness can be replicated. Do it again and make being aware of joyful things a habit.

This work sets the Universe in motion to bring you the happiness you desire. You are working to change your paradigm and although you generally desire instantaneous results, the effort might take some time depending on how strongly positioned and fearful you are of change. Your beliefs concerning your possibilities for happiness are also part of your vibration and these can be powerful limitations as well. Beliefs and the part they play in your life are addressed in Chapters 4 through 8.

As with the establishment of most habits (yes, you want awareness to become a habit!), it helps if there is some stimulus to get you started. Choose a trigger. Perhaps first thing in the morning (opening your eyes?) and say out loud "Today I choose to be happy". As you say it, feel the happiness you seek and then, as Captain Picard in *Star Trek*, says - including the outstretched pointing finger - "Make it So". With this you are saying to the Universe, "I am the captain of my ship and this is what I want." It cements your intention as creator of your own reality, and significantly raises your vibration.

In *Illusions*, Richard Bach writes:

> "You are
> never given a wish
> without also being given the
> power to make it true.
> You may
> have to work for it,
> however."

Start this work immediately and make it a habit. Below are some other possibilities you may want to add to your choosing:

Today I choose to be the Love that I AM.
Today I choose to be at Peace with all that is.
Today I choose to be aware.
Today I choose to have fun.
Today I choose to trust and allow.

The Universe needs some general directions. Being "happy" is a sufficiency, however, there is a possibility that you might want to add a little structure to your creational desires. It is important if you want to take this step that you make all of these ideas your own and not simply repeat them as one might in a ritual. Feel them and the truth of your really having them and see yourself in situations where they have already come to pass.

Overall there might be a guiding intention of your life. It can be anything. The Universe does not care. For some it might be that however you manifest, it be for the Highest Good of all concerned. Everything must fit comfortably into this intention.

Under that there might be "druthers". These are desires, but not requirements, and can come to pass as they will, as long as they fit the overall intention. They are, as you will see, general in nature for the same reasons that being happy is left general - the Universe is given freedom to bring them to pass in the best synergy for you.

Some "druthers" might be:

1. Freedom to be, do and have anything you choose.
2. The Great and Little abundance in unlimited quantity.

The "Great" abundance is Joy, Love, Happiness and Peace. The "Little" abundance is money and/or the things it can provide. Here we're talking about great goo-gobs.

3. Wondrous, healthy physicality. Young, vibrant, alive, great energy.
4. A wonderful interpersonal relationship on the physical, emotional, mental and spiritual level.

In all this visualization work, it is <u>extremely</u> important NOT to be attached to the outcome of anything. Your desire is the only work that needs to be done. All attachment to the outcome has a fear base that it won't or isn't happening, and what you will get is the fear portion of the creating vibration. This is because the fear is the more energetic creational energy. It is also important to know that too much "wanting" results in the "wanting" being created and not the outcome.

The primary causative human vibrational energy on earth is emotional. For most, decisions are made emotionally, and then justified by our intellect.

Begin the work NOW.

"Who" you are has been defined as the point of consciousness in the present that is the Love of the Universe. How you might like to manifest is your choice. We include here a poem by Rudyard Kipling that might ring true for you in it's general concept of how a person might want to express themselves. Although it is written for a son, it can obviously pertain to either sex.

IF
by
Rudyard Kipling

If you can keep your head, when all about you
Are losing theirs and blaming it on you,
If you can trust yourself, when all men doubt you,
But make allowance for their doubting too;
If you can wait and not be tired by waiting,
Or being lied about, don't deal in lies,
Or being hated, don't give way to hating,
And yet, don't look too good, nor talk too wise:

If you can dream - and not make dreams your master;
If you can think - and not make thoughts your aim;
If you can meet with Triumph and Disaster
And treat those two impostors just the same;
If you can bear to hear the truth you've spoken
Twisted by Knaves to make a trap for fools,
Or watch the things you gave your life to broken,
And stoop and build 'em up with worn-out tools:

If you can make one heap of all your winnings
And risk it on one turn of pitch and toss,

And loose and start again at your beginnings
And never breath a word about your loss;
If you can force your heart and nerve and sinew
To serve your turn long after they are gone,
And so hold on, when there is nothing in you
Except the Will which says to them: "Hold on!"

If you can talk with crowds and keep you virtue,
Or walk with kings - nor loose the common touch,
If neither foes nor loving friends can hurt you,
If all men count with you, but none too much;
If you can fill the unforgiving minute
With sixty seconds' worth of distance run,
Yours is the Earth and everything that's in it,
And - what is more - you'll be a Man, my son.

Having set all this in motion, let's put together some tools and information that will help you to further embrace the concept, remove limitations and feel more comfortable in changing your reality.

There is a major concept to keep in mind as we get into the work. It has been mentioned before, however, it is very important and worth mentioning again. Everything is cyclical. There will be times of growth and times of seeming to move backwards. Be OK with this. Patience. Your intent insures forward motion.

Note: "If" by Rudyard Kipling is in the public domain.

Chapter 4

TOOLS

I'VE WORKED HARD AT CHANGING, YET THINGS STAY THE SAME. WHY?

The simple answer is your programming, which generates your vibration from the sources listed in Chapter 2. The next most important reason is because we live in time, and it took years to create your current reality and may (or may not) take years to change it to what you want.

As a result of these two reasons, the most necessary ingredient in the change mix is patience. Patience is not a natural human capability, it is learned.

This chapter addresses potential causes and limitations for continuing unhappiness and how to remove their effects.

It takes work. This chapter is the "work", assuming you have the ingredients mentioned in Chapter 1: Desire, Persistence, Awareness and, of course, Patience.

There is a <u>VERY</u> important point to remind yourself of at this juncture:

The work is emotional.
The releases are emotional.
The intellect is only the guide.

Don Shimoda, in Richard Bach's *Illusions,* offers that there are two simultaneous games going on here in Earth. One is to learn and the other is to have fun. We are doing the first all the time and seeking the second. They are, and can be, simultaneous goals. Can you imagine if our learning from here on were ALSO fun? "I Choose to have fun" is one of our potential program instructions to the Universe, remember? What a concept. What a reality.

In *Illusions*, Richard Bach also writes:

Perspective -
Use it or lose it.

One of the most important tools of a happy life is being able to bring perspective to situations. It is one of the goals of this book to put the understandings of life in a sufficiently logical manner to be able to have perspective as an automatic response.

To have this, one must understand the various components and possibilities that surround existing behavior as well as desired changes. Knowledge and understanding are what bring perspective, so a good deal of what is shared in this book is knowledge that leads through a "logical" pathway to allow for emotional releases. The knowledge provides a background understanding of how things work so that you can believe at a conscious level that taking the actions recommended here will have the desired effects.

Perspective can be fun as well as informative. Many of you have been exposed to the ideas concerning the difference between left-brain and right-brain approaches to your world.

It concerns the differences between left-brain and right brain functions. The left-brain is the male, reasoning, scientific, etc. side of our brain. The right brain is the female, emotional, intuitive, creative side. Both sides have their "logic" and herein lies a problem. Emotional "logic" is very different from intellectual "logic", and one of the major problems between the sexes is that a women's emotional logic can drive men crazy because it isn't "logical". Similarly, men's reasoning "logic" can drive a woman crazy for the same reason.

It can be of considerable help in understanding and dealing with this difference when doing almost anything with another person. It can also help in dealing with your internal reactions with your self.

It is also a good idea to remember that "irrational" behavior is not "irrational" to the person exhibiting it. Can you relate to what is going on in such a person's world?

We all have both left and right brains, obviously. Some men are more in tune with their "feminine" side and some women are more in tune with their "masculine" side. Most people are well balanced, but even in this case when a man is thinking from the left-brain and a women interjects an emotional component, it can be, at the least, disquieting. Likewise, for a woman who is being creative, a man's logic, at that time, is annoying. This dichotomy can exists within yourself and this sometimes can create confusion. The point is made solely that you can become aware and have more understanding of what is really going on. "Knowledge is power".

Many men don't speak "woman" and many women don't speak "man". Think about this. It could make your ability to function with the opposite sex MUCH easier. After all, it makes it all "logical". This dichotomy does not necessarily exist only between the sexes, but is common-enough in man-man and woman-woman interactions as well.

It does require an effort to "think" in a different modality, and while you may come to understand it, that doesn't mean it becomes your way of thinking. It is called "empathy".

Let me share a personal experience here. I was tiling a bathroom and was short on tiles by only one. In the lot of tiles I had bought there was one orange tile among the brown ones. I installed it behind where the bath vanity was to go. Perfectly "logical" to me. The person for whom I was doing the work became upset because of this anomaly. I said it would never be seen and they said it didn't matter, they would know it was there. Totally, totally, TOTALLY outside my ability to understand from my left-brain.

I called a girlfriend in another state and told her the story and she agreed! Unbelievable! A totally "illogical" response.

The tile remained. So male!

With this as a starting point in "perspective", there is a great deal that needs to be brought into the light about this point. The importance of it will be emphasized many times as we move forward.

The new perspective says that what is present is perfect for each person and each person's reality is theirs, not yours. It says very clearly that we created all of this and brought it to ourselves. There is no one to "blame" for our reality except us. Yet in any situation there is no "blame" for us either, because we did, and are doing, the best we can with what we have. We are therefore willing to assume total responsibility for what is in our lives and make changes without beating up on ourselves. There is a wonderful saying when we begin to get too involved in others lives and accept their problems as ours. It is:

> It's not my pig.
> It's not my farm.

And one more:

> You cannot assume responsibility for
> anyone's life
> but your own.

There are a couple of other important changes in perspective that are worth knowing. They are:

> TANA.

There Are No Accidents.

> That's not the nature of
> Consciousness.

And

> You can never be late.

You can be not on time, but in the realm of cosmic purpose, your lateness is Perfect. It gives all involved (including yourself) an opportunity to look at what is going on or has gone on. Is there something to be gained from this behavior and do you like the results?

And a big one:

> Everyone is doing exactly what they
> came to do. All ways.

Each person is in the perfect place to accomplish their learning, regardless of your opinion of their actions. Accept this and you have made a huge step in letting others live their own lives, and allowing yourself to be at peace with what's going on. As mentioned before, all is choice.

The new perspective also calls for a change in attitude. What appears to be problems are not problems, they are opportunities we have created to bring to ourselves the happiness we seek. The Universe MUST bring us our stated desires and therefore whatever happens is ABSOLUTELY on the path to achieving that goal. Everything is a stimulus for change in the directions we have now consciously chosen and we CREATED it.

It is very important to remember that those we have come in contact with in our experiences have also attracted us to them. The mutual attraction provides each a gift that is most likely not the same for both parties. The opportunity provided for growth may also not be taken by either or both parties. If not taken, then the "opportunity" will be presented again - perhaps this time more powerfully to get your (their) attention.

In this context, even if you have done something "bad" (we'll get to this concept later), the person you have done the "bad" to attracted you to them to experience the "bad" so they can have their potential learning.

Regarding questions you have. When you ask a question it has a vibration. This "vibration" automatically attracts the answer to you through the law of "Like Vibrations Attract". If you remember this when you ask a question, it can help in realizing the answer is available. You may need to "look" for it using your tools.

There is a question that usually arises here about those born with "defects", genetic predispositions and things that happen to children who seem unable to create circumstances that are damaging. At this juncture it is important that we address "normal" conditions and will get to the circumstances surrounding these situations in Chapters 9 and 10.

Once again in *Illusions*, Richard Bach puts it succinctly:

> "There is
> no such thing as a problem
> without a gift for you
> in its hands.
> You seek problems
> because you need
> their gifts."

What is the "gift" your problem has for you?

What is the "gift" of each of your parents, siblings, friends, constituents, antagonists and partners? How has their involvement in your life changed you in the direction you chose? What have you learned - not to avoid them, but to perhaps accept and thank them for your involvement. You may be surprised at the answers from the new perspective.

It is worthwhile to ask yourself that question when dealing with any problem.

"What is the gift?"

One of the greatest "gifts" we are given as humans is fear. How strange does that sound? Fear is something we try to avoid and it is actually the only limitation we have to being free to be, do and have anything we choose. So how is fear a gift?

Two ways:

First: It keeps you safe from perceived "danger" in certain potential events. The reptilian brain is the keeper of the fear response and is hard- wired into the human psyche for survival.

Second: It is a doorway to the changes we wish to make in order to achieve our desired happiness and peace.

It is this second part that we will address with tools to identify and release the automatic responses we have in the first part.

Another great "gift" is behavior patterns. Here we have the opportunity to recognize patterns that we want to change and can again apply tools to achieve those ends.

So much philosophy, you might say, and where are the "tools"?

The "philosophy" shared is an integral part of the foundation of how you can look at the situations of life and keep perspective. Changing your philosophy allows the filter through which you look at life to broaden and perhaps make the reactions to change less fearful.

Here we introduce one of the most important concepts/tools in the book. It is:

You live to serve your belief systems.

In chapter 1, we talk about the "box" in which you live. The floor of this box is said to be your beliefs based on your experiences and genetic programming. In order to keep you "safe" you have built walls of behaviors that limit you in your life. Some useful, some not. Our purpose is to remove those that are "not" which are operative in your life today.

If you "believe" something to be true, you have created as part of your vibration that certainty and the Universe will respond by bringing forth that which supports your belief. This is a very broad concept. Belief that you are "unworthy", "haven't earned what you want", "don't deserve whatever it is you desire", and so many more pre-conceived notions, automatically limits you in moving into the reality you are working to achieve.

Poor self worth is the most prevalent belief most of us harbor. It has usefulness as we grow up at times because it causes us to stretch and work to be more than we think we are in the moment. As an adult, however, it is a meaningless term. Who is judging you as "good enough"? You are. Is anyone else who matters doing this and are you buying it? Have you given your power to someone else to decide whether you have sufficient "value" to have "earned" some thing or some place in society or some acknowledgement that validates your worth? The Universe certainly doesn't judge you, YOU do. The "American Dream" that is talked about so much is basically the freedom to rise above the limitations set by a rigid society. We are taught that we all have the opportunities to improve our lot, yet many of us accept our "place in life" and never question it. Who says you can't fulfill your dreams? In this expanded reality, it is only you who makes that decision. "Worth" is determined internally, not externally. No one who counts judges you except you.

As mentioned in Chapter 1, one of the most prevalent behavior filters a child expresses comes from the "black and white", and "all or nothing" absoluteness of early growth. This exists because of the natural limitations of the brain at those ages. For most, this remains an active cornerstone and limitation of our potential changes in attitudes and actions. Our first reactions are often "no". Then the rest of the programming may cut in and allow you to think. But often it does not, and the "absoluteness programming" makes your choices for you. It helps to be aware of your initial responses.

We seek validation of our behaviors as children and seldom give up looking for that from others as we grow. It can be validation of your value, but it can also be to reinforce your attitude that you are not worthy. Take a look at what you seek from others as validation. Take over that responsibility and validate yourself. Starting NOW!

At this point it is worth mentioning one of the most confusing and difficult situations we have as humans and put it in the perspective of beliefs and good and bad feelings. Relationships is the subject.

Change Your Reality

We all have experiences with relationships. The most interesting, compelling and confusing one involves falling and being in love with another person. Here is a scenario that probably sounds familiar.

You fall in love and it feels really good. Time passes and you have fights and maybe fall out of love and break up and it feels really bad. You come up with a series of beliefs as a result which say certain things such as I want this or I want that or I DON'T want this, etc. Then, after the next one that also "fails" you come to believe that relationships just aren't for you because you are too:

SOMETHING

Such as:

Sensitive.
Picky.
Old.
Different.
Unattractive.
Beautiful.
Hairy.
Good.
Bad.
Rich.
Poor.
Emotionally unstable.
Emotionally stable.
Unfit (whatever that means).
and on and on and ON.

Then there is the list of characteristics and traits that you think you do or do not now require. That the partner is:

SOMETHING

Such as:

Too tall.
Too short.
Must love to dance or cook, like sports or music, etc. or maybe none of these.
Must like going to concerts.
Must have great sense of humor.
Must be innocent and child-like.
Must not be too touchy-feely.
Must be very touchy-feely.
Must be gorgeous, but not too.
Must have money.
Must not have money.

How many do you need? Each person can make a list twice as long as this.

The fact is that one becomes seriously conflicted, both wanting and not wanting a relationship at the same time. What's a body to do?

Here is the new approach:

> "Universe, I want a Perfect relationship
> and I don't have a clue what that means.
> I leave it to you,
> Thanks."

There are many factors that contribute to the subject of "relationships". They include the beliefs surrounding the subject, survival responses in not wanting to get hurt again, the considerable uncomfortableness that comes up when even mentioning the subject and conclusions arrived at such as "I'm simply much happier without having to compromise". There are others, but the whole idea is that first you need to make the choice as to whether you do want a relationship and if you do, then instruct the Universe to bring you one and let go. It may take a while. Most people have lots of "stuff" surrounding having a relationship that needs to be addressed and removed before the Perfect Relationship can arrive.

Regarding dealing with beliefs, here is a specific "tool" that can be used to change existing programming. It is called:

The Circle of Experience

This is a significant tool you can use to address and release many limiting belief systems.

We, as humans, operate from experiences that generate behavior patterns that result in predictable responses to stimuli. We have very little conscious space (remember the 40 to 20,000,000 ratio in Chapter 1?), so almost all of our actions are non-conscious behavior patterns set in motion by some stimuli (I'm thirsty, hot, driving, watching TV, whatever).

The belief plays the part of channeling a potential triggering event through internal "check points" into a path that will result in a particular response (perhaps fear, perhaps not - it works on all triggers). Here is an example of how most of the beliefs resulting from this life are generated.

As a child, you go out in the rain without your galoshes (do any of you know what "galoshes" are?). You come back in with wet feet and your mother changes your socks and shoes. The next day you come down with a cold. Mother tells you that you got the cold because you went out without your galoshes. She is "all knowing", so she is <u>right</u>, and next time you go out without your galoshes you get another cold. Why? Because you have now accepted as part of your experience that this is the way it is. That you got a cold the first time may or may not have had anything to do with getting your feet wet, but every time after that first experience, the causal factor will be the belief you accepted regarding galoshes, rain and getting a cold.

The "inevitable" spring cold is another example of "old wives tales" running our lives. The cold has nothing to do with spring. It was totally created as a result of the belief. Likewise for walking under ladders, throwing salt over your shoulder, and such.

A circle of experience has been created in which the triggering event is rain, no galoshes and the resulting cold. To break the circle of experience it is only necessary to remove the absoluteness of the circle. Like so:

Ask yourself:

"Is it <u>NECESSARILY</u> true that not wearing galoshes in the rain will give me a cold?"

In a calm manner you only have to acknowledge and FEEL that no - it is not <u>NECESSARILY</u> true. You need to identify only one experience within or outside yourself in which this "truth" has been shown not to be true and the circle is then broken.

It's that easy.

There are obviously millions of people who go out in the rain without their galoshes and don't get colds. A large number of which don't have a clue what galoshes are.

Of course you must feel the truth of your new insight. Pretending won't work. There is almost always someone or something that has had a different outcome from one of your experientially-programmed responses and resulting beliefs.

There is a very important point to make here that you need to remember:

> All beliefs, no matter their source,
> are available to the conscious mind.

What this says is that whether the belief originates from genetics, this life, other lives or wherever, you do not have to search for their source to change them. They are all there in your synaptic/cellular memory. You don't need therapy, other life investigation or any other methodology to bring up the belief. This does not invalidate therapy or looking into other lives if that is a path you choose to follow. It simply says that if you are patient and honest with yourself, the driving belief behind some action is available to the conscious mind now.

Some of the most powerful imbedded beliefs are the result of vows taken under stress or with great intent. These vows can be all inclusive, that is span the breadth of all your activities, or be very specific. Here are several examples:

All vows coming from religious affiliation.
Not allow yourself to have money.
Never trust God again.
Be a know-it-all.
Have power.
Have children.
Care.
Be committed to a "cause".

Each of these, and any others that you might have, can be released in their "absoluteness" through using the "circle of experience" or one of the other "tools" shared in this chapter.

Railing at God is a normal reaction for us when we hurt. The child wants to blame and "punish back" that which we perceive is the hurtful one or thing that has betrayed us.

Perspective is called for here. First that it is OK, because we are human, and second because it offers us an opportunity to bring about desired change. If you can come to accept that it is you who created this situation, then you can also let yourself off the hook because it was just experience with a potential for learning and growing.

Here is another "tool" that may be of use to you. It involves repeating the accusatory statement again and again with increasing energy. Such as: "I am stupid". I am <u>really</u> stupid. I am stupid beyond belief. YES, I AM terminally stupid - etc., getting more and more energetic as you keep telling yourself that you are stupid.

You start this exercise with the INTENT of releasing the belief. Eventually, when you keep it up, you begin to feel the real truth that this just isn't so. Ridiculous! It may take a while, but sometimes it works. Sometimes all it does is make it worse, even though your logical side says that it is impossible that EVERYTHING you have ever done is stupid.

If this does not work, the resulting question would be "Why is it so important for me to KNOW that I am stupid?" Am I afraid of being smart? Why? Your imagination and intuition will take you to the place where you can truly FEEL that you are NOT terminally stupid.

This approach can also be used when you are afraid of something and you don't know what it is. In this case you again set your intent. Then you would continue to say "I am afraid" many times working to feel the cause behind the feeling. If it becomes obvious that this approach only makes things worse, stop. This is not your path to release. There will be others. The reason we know this is because you have set your vibrational intent to release the fear and the Universal computer will do as it has been instructed.

There are two systems you might try to see if they can work for you. They both provide an insight into your own internal operating systems.

The first is called Applied Kinesiology. It uses the body's response to stimuli at a strictly physical level. As an example, one might hold a pill or a bottle of pills of some kind in your hand and test it using a kinesiological approach to see if your body "likes" it or not. There are several systems that can work and some of you will know them. I offer here a system that has worked for me (it takes practice and an earning of trust to put full confidence in it). It is another useful "tool".

Whether you are left or right handed makes no difference. I shall give instructions as if you were right handed. For left-handed people just reverse the hands.

First, practice without holding anything in your hand. Hold your right hand with the palm up and bend the finger next to your pinky (the ring finger) up to a vertical position and curl it back toward yourself. The tip should now be pointing back towards you. Say the word "resist" and put the tip in tension. Now, with the thumb of the other hand, push on it to make it move away from you. It should remain relatively unmoved. Now relax the tip and push it away from you (again with the thumb of the other hand) and note the difference. In the relaxed mode the finger should move easily. When you say "resist" and put tension on the tip of the finger, you do not have to hurt it. It is not necessary to injure the finger to use the system. Practice will show you the level of resistance that answers your question. The difference is easy to discern without damage. Try both conditions a couple of times to get the hang of it.

Next, try the system first with something that you know is good for you and also something you know is not.

Holding the item (if it is not possible to hold it, concentrate visually upon it, or if that is not possible picture it) and place the thumb of the opposite hand at the tip. Say the word "resist" and tense the ring finger to keep it from moving. Apply pressure from the thumb of the other hand to push the ring finger away from you. Keep resisting the straightening with the ring finger. If the finger resists being pushed away, then the answer is "it is good for me", If it moves relatively easily (remember to keep tension on it as if you are resisting), then the body is saying that this item is not good for me, it makes me "weak". Little movement is saying "yes" (strong). Lots of movement is saying "no" (weak).

This will take some practice but eventually you can become comfortable with it. Every once in a while test it on things you know the answer to just to check whether the non-conscious may be playing it's own game. Such as, "Is this large bag of M&Ms good for me?" and the answer is "yes". Feel the truth of the answer as you get it, and if the "truth" is really that the large bag of M&Ms is good for you, then begin eating. Eventually you might be able to "intuit" the correct answer as you ask.

<u>Always check your answer with your logic.</u>

Those with control issues may have some initial problem "letting go". Work on it. Put your mind in "neutral" and confirm that you don't know the right answer, otherwise you wouldn't be asking a question! Focus on the word "resist" and on the finger, not the question, after you have stated the question.

Remember: It is NOT necessary to push too hard to get an answer! Find your right "resistance" level.

The second system is using the pendulum. This too takes some practice to become comfortable with the answer.

The pendulum can be used for many purposes, including determining simple answers such as "yes", "no" and "I don't know". Many of you are familiar with this "tool" and are aware that successful use depends on the intent of the user. Setting the "intent" is vital to be able to effectively assist in this kind of work. The "intent" in this case is to set up a communications link with your "non-conscious" self.

The use of the pendulum can be very frustrating because the answers you get are a function of your non-consciousness and not necessarily the final/total "truth" you seek, but simply a first step in that direction. At the same time it IS the "truth" of your non-consciousness, so considerable discernment and awareness are necessary to get answers that lead you to the information you desire. Take no answer as "absolute" truth, but as a path to learning more about what is going on and eventual release of undesired beliefs and behavior patterns. Often when you arrive at the "truth" there will be an "ah-ha" moment and resultant feeling. Watch for it.

It is important to remember that your non-consciousness may have an answer with which you do not agree. Don't simply discard it because you can't believe you believe whatever it is you have just brought forward. On the surface you may not believe what you have just found out, but whatever it is needs to be brought forward to be looked at and potentially released.

The device itself is a simple weighted string about 6-9 inches long. The weight can be anything. I have them everywhere made out of all kinds of items but the one I use the most is my car keys on a ring with a cut piece of shoestring. There are 3 or 4 keys on the ring at a time, to give you an idea of a good weight to use. You will arrive at something that works for you, however, it must have SOME heft, otherwise it won't swing. Using the shoestring on the key ring also makes it easier for me to get them out of my pocket. Sometimes everything else comes with them, but that's another story.

The pendulum works through small movements in directions you determine, to answer discreet questions requiring primarily "yes" and "no" answers. It is up to you to form the questions so that they are not ambiguous and the answers are clear. One of the most valuable aspects of using the pendulum is the requirement to come up with clear questions that put your thoughts in a more precise context. In fact, it is the most significant step in learning about your self.

The idea behind using the pendulum is that all our physical movements are controlled by our internal programming and thus, in this case, potentially out of our conscious control.

If you have not used a pendulum before, you are in for a surprise. I showed it to one friend and they immediately backed away and put it down. Their quote was "I didn't do that!" And that was the end of their using the pendulum. Of course they DID do that and the fact that they didn't consciously control it, and it happened anyway, and they freaked, speaks gobs. As everything else, if you let it work and don't throw up fear blockages about it, it CAN be a useful adjunct to your process.

The important point is that it is YOU answering and not someone else. It is just an aspect of yourself that usually makes itself known through other mechanisms, such as making you think of something that you have no idea "where that came from". "The Freudian Slip" is from this place as well as are internal songs. How nice to be able to access it consciously. It is neither an enemy nor a stranger. You have known yourself at this level forever. Consider it the keeper of the feelings. It has been called the inner child but it is really the automatic set of behavior patterns that is you. Sometimes you will get answers that you don't expect. That's great. It is an opening to self-understanding. The goal in using the pendulum is the same as the goal in the process - to bring into harmony your non-conscious self with your conscious aspect. This is a potential window.

It is important here to note, that if for some reason it does not work for you or you feel very uncomfortable about it, then don't do it. It is NOT critical and sometimes only adds to the confusion. In using the pendulum you need to be on your intellectual toes. Keep that in mind.

The first step is to make the pendulum. You've hopefully done that. If you decide to make a "special" one, that's fine, but for the start, anything that approximately fits the above description will work. Next, hold it between the thumb and four-finger of which ever hand you write with, place your elbow on a non-moving surface and let it hang down about 5-6 inches. Consciously make it swing from left to right. Tell yourself consciously, as you are swinging it, that this direction is "no". Stop it moving and consciously swing it towards and away from your body. Tell yourself that this direction is "yes". Again stop it and consciously swing it in a circle counter clockwise and tell yourself that this means "I don't know" or "maybe". The final direction, circling clockwise, can mean anything you want to label it. I have come to call this an "I got it" response. This means when internally I have changed my mind and the issue has "been addressed", then this movement says "I got it". You can use any variation you desire but once the directions are established, be consistent.

Now, the simplest way to try it out is to let it dangle and try not to make it move. Don't stop it from moving; just don't "make up" the answer for yourself. Just watch. This is pivotal. JUST WATCH.

Let's begin with a simple example:

Having taught yourself the meaning of the movements, hold the pendulum as suggested and let it be at rest. Ask yourself if your name is something other than your real name. It might go something like this:

Q: Is my name Steve? (Angela?)

A: (hopefully) no.

Q: Is it (your real name)?
A: Yes.

This will let you know whether you are ready to start using it in earnest. If the answers are not as expected, then you can proceed to ask such questions as shown below concerning fears about its use.

A couple of rules:

1. Stay consciously aware of what is going on. Don't "give yourself up" to the answers. You must stay in a state of questioning and feeling what is happening. Sometimes you will know some answer is made up. It will just feel like it. Note that. And proceed accordingly. There is an example of this below.
2. Keep your power in the present.

The next step might be as follows:
Q: Do we want to communicate in this manner?
A: Yes. Then proceed in using it.
or:
A: No.

If it is in the "no" direction, in reality you have already started communicating and you can pursue the reason why this is the case.

or:
A: No movement.

If there remains no movement, then the pendulum is not going to work for you at this time; there is too much concern about knowing the truth or letting go of control. You might come back at a later time and try again.

The movement, especially at first, will be tentative and small. It will seldom be great, and you will be able to discern the answers by direction relatively soon. Always watch the pendulum when using it - the visual feedback is necessary to make the system work. Try to relax and not pre-determine the answers. Just let it hang and "do it's thing". Now comes the hard part. Using it so that you learn something, rather than run yourself around in circles. After all it is you, and who is smarter, you or you?

Keep in mind that the cornerstone of this system working is that there is no enemy. It is you and you, each doing the best with what they have and each coming from their own (but intermingled) experiences on both sides of the consciousness fence.

The following might be a continuation of the pursuit of using the pendulum comfortably.

First establish the starting point by thinking to yourself:
Q: "I don't seem to want to use the pendulum."
A: A "yes" motion confirms this.
Then the question:
Q: Do I know why?

There may or may not be an answer. The fact that there was a "yes" response indicates that the system at least works and there is the potential of trying again some time. If there is none, then, as before, perhaps we need to leave this tool alone for a while and come back another time. If the answer is "yes", then we have begun a potential learning opportunity.

A: Yes.
Q: I am afraid? (This is the statement that starts the process. There is a very high probability that this is the case, however, there are other possibilities, such as: "I don't want to play [I feel powerless]", or "I can't deal with this"; "I feel inept", or perhaps some other reason. Let us assume the answer is:
A: Yes.
Q: Do I know what the reason I am afraid is?
A: Yes.

Bring something to mind. I can feel the fear, but I can't label it.

Q: Am I afraid of the "truth"?
A: No.

Q: Am I afraid that I, who am asking the questions, won't like the answers?
A: Yes.

OK. (Statement of intent to self). "I know that I have been hard on myself for all these years and doubt my honesty when I say I'm not going to be judgmental, however, I am going to do my best to change that pattern and need all the internal help I can get to do this. I realize that I am a function of everything that has happened to me and there is nothing wrong with me and I shall NOT come down on myself if I don't like the answer."

Can we continue?
A: First a "maybe", changing to a "tentative" yes.

(As you progress, you will be able to notice subtle differences in the answers. Sometimes enthusiastic, sometimes small and cautious.)

That's a great start.

Q: Is there anything else I am afraid of?
A: Yes.

Q: Am I afraid I will be punished if I give the wrong answers?
A: No.

Q: Am I afraid I won't be liked?
A: No.

Q: Am I afraid of the magic?
A: Yes.

I am afraid of the magic. (This is a statement to focus on the next question.)

Q: Does this mean that having this power scares me?
A: Yes.

Q: What do I believe that the magic frightens me?
A: I can't handle magic. (This is a thought)
Q: Then what I am really saying is that I feel inadequate to deal with this situation, I feel inept?
A: Yes.
Q: So I believe that I am inept?
A: Yes.
Q: Is that absolutely true? Am I "inept" at everything?
A: (perhaps) Yes.

With this response one might say. "Really? Everything! Is that really true? How about drinking water?" (Or something very simple which few if any can not do well.)

Then one might say:

Q: So it isn't true that I am not good (inept) at everything, is it?
A: No.
Q: So do I still believe that I am not good at anything?
A: No.

If the answer is yes, then find something that you are good at - anything - and keep at it until the answer is "No, I no longer believe I am inept at everything."

Here, you go into convincing yourself that it is OK to proceed. Remember that you are addressing the inner patterns of your own psyche. While the statement below has great similarities with the one above concerning intent, it is definitively worth repeating at this stage of process. You might do it something like this:

Statement: I no longer am going to judge any aspect of myself as being good or bad. It is all just experience that occurred during this life or others and led me to where I am. I have always been able to deal with life to some degree and although I fully understand that I seldom felt it was done well, it nonetheless was done and the measure of success is that I am here now and working at changing. I am capable of moving forward, even though in small steps, and promise to have patience with myself and work at not being angry. When I am, as I have been in the past, I shall stop, because I realize it is destructive and gets me nowhere. I realize that I am coming from lots of behavior patterns and these are not who I am but sometimes I cannot help it. I promise to know that whatever occurs, the internal me is not to "blame", for I am simply being me. It is only through working with my total self that I can get anywhere and be at peace with myself.

Note: This is very wordy, however, for purposes of assisting in covering many bases, it contains several potentially useful points. Make it your own with your own thoughts and words.

Q: Am I willing to work with the pendulum in this context to make my life better?

A: Maybe.

Statement to yourself: OK, That's good enough for now. I'm going to stop and come back later. This is a very powerful tool and it scares me a little. I need to let some of this "sink in" and become more comfortable.

An important point to remember in this process is that the mind is a hologram. It takes time to integrate new concepts and ideas. Personally, when I have come to a significant understanding I "back off" for the rest of the day and go on about the business of living. Believe it or not, there is no hurry, for you WILL get there. One step at a time. Patience with yourself - always and all ways.

The question may arise as to whether it is appropriate to name the energy moving the pendulum. In order to avoid additional separations, I have come to use the term "I". This acknowledges that it is indeed me who is operating the pendulum from whatever level the information comes and it is indeed me I am working with. At no time is it to be thought of as a separate person, it is simply another expression of you.

The answers come from patterns and personality that you use to express your beingness in life. Keep in mind that you are now and ever have been a single point of consciousness passing through the element we call time. To label the energy as a child is not correct, for you will be addressing yourself at many ages and perhaps many lifetimes. I shall give several examples below. Pay attention to the tenor of the approach.

One of the most significant points to remember during this process is that there are few subjects that don't have multiple answers. It can be: I like it at one level and I don't at another. As a simple example, you didn't like some foods at age 5 that you love now. Perhaps you've come to like ham and pineapple on pizza.

The greatest use I found for it is labeling what it is that really bothered me about an incident. I will consciously think it is one thing and will work the pendulum and come up with it being something else. When I do get the "right" answer, I emotionally recognize it immediately and proceed accordingly. Which leads to a very real question:

How do you know when the pendulum is telling the "truth"?

It is always telling the truth, but the "truth" of the inner self may be in conflict with your conscious "truth". What you are asking may be counter to what you can reveal to yourself, because at some level you are frightened to know the "truth". This is a very common situation, for what we may "know" as the truth is in fact that we are useless, powerless, unlovable and inept at dealing with life. The truth in the past has not set us free. On the contrary, to us it has often seemed dangerous. The truth WILL set you free, however, the difficulty arises in discerning what is real and what is manufactured. Only having the real truth can allow you to make beneficial decisions.

Think of a time in which the "truth" actually was painful. This shouldn't be too hard. Look at that situation from today's perspective and see if your actually accepting that "truth" might have changed what you perceived to be a negative outcome. The challenge is to really want emotionally to know the truth so that you can change your reality in a way you choose. Sometimes this emotional change of attitude can be difficult. By being consistent that you do indeed want the real "truth" this attitude will change.

Another conflict in using the pendulum can come from what sometimes appears to be an illogical answer. In this instance, it could be coming from "magical thinking".

A worthwhile thought to keep in mind is that if what is happening appears to be illogical, then you simply do not understand the logic, for everything makes sense to the individual who is doing the doing. Even if it is "you" who is being illogical with you. Also be aware that emotional "logic" is not necessarily intellectual "logic".

ALWAYS keep in mind that you are speaking to your patterns and programmed personality. It was never who you really were, nor who you are now, but it can help you to clear out the patterns that are limiting your freedom.

Remember too, you are a point of consciousness in the present and always have been just that. At each moment in that "present" you are the cumulative expression of all your experiences and thus the only "real" you. This continues for your whole life. You, in the present, are therefore, by definition, the best "you" to make decisions and be the boss. This is because you (again in the present) have the most experience in living and therefore have the best database for making decisions.

A child's experiences are limited by time.
An adult knows much more.
Thus the adult, you in the present, are the best decision maker.

THE POINT OF POWER IS ONLY IN THE PRESENT.

Change Your Reality

Remember, both of these systems are bringing forth answers from the non-conscious level and need to be checked against the logic of the response.

The primary stimulus for finding these beliefs is your emotional reaction to your world.

Here is one of many techniques used for finding the core beliefs:

Let us say that you just did something that you don't find to your liking, such as getting real hot under the collar when someone said something. It might not even have been directed at you, but you had an emotional reaction.

This is the first clue - an <u>emotional</u> reaction. This is the stimulus to begin your work.

Ask yourself "What do I believe that _____?"

Such as " What do I believe that <u>I just had THAT reaction?</u>"

Here is a powerful personal example of "what was THAT" and the resultant awareness for me.

I was driving down the Taconic Parkway in New York and moving along at 70. This was well above the speed limit. I was passing another car and looked in my rear view mirror and saw that someone was coming up on me at a rapid rate (it was not a policeman). He got closer and closer to my bumper and as he did my adrenalin began to flow. Within seconds I was furious and ready to slam on the brakes regardless of what would happen. I was totally in the "fight" mode. Somehow I managed to keep my speed constant and as I passed the car I was passing, I pulled over to the right and he zoomed past. My blood pressure had to be through the roof. I seldom have this kind of reaction and I didn't care what happened to me, or my car! DIDN'T CARE!!!!! FURIOUS!! OVER THE TOP!! I'D SHOW THE M...F...!!

Got the idea?

It took several miles to cool down enough to realize that the incident was a gift and address the reaction and ask:

"What was THAT about?"

My reaction was that he was "saying" to me, through his actions, that I was nothing. Absolutely useless, and to get out of his way. What I asked myself was did I believe that I was nothing?, useless?, less than anything and everything? The answer was yes. He was telling me my "truth" and I didn't like it AT ALL (we seldom do).

Regardless of the source, I believed I was valueless, useless and all of those things, and he was telling me my truth. How DARE he. Addressing it was a matter of breaking the circle of experience by saying "Is it true that I am terminally useless/nothing/etc.?" The answer was "no", and eventually I calmed down even to the point of blessing him for the "gift" of the experience, insight and release.

The next part of the release is to ask yourself if you are ever useless (etc.). The answer is yes, sometimes, but SO WHAT! That trait is an integral part of what I am and I like me – a lot. So, once in a while, being useless is quite OK! This concept is covered in more detail later in this chapter.

There is another "tool" that can be used when asking a question. It is particularly useful when wanting to know why or how something works. It is imaging - allowing images or ideas to come to mind as the answer to your question. The actual answer comes in the form of what is called a "light pictograph". Once I give the example below, you will get a feeling of when this tool might be useful. This is an example that actually occurred for me.

The question was: "Why does a nail that has been blunted by hitting the pointy end with a hammer not split the wood when turned around the right way and hammered into a board?"

The answer instantly came as a complete informational packet. I knew the answer and all the things that made it true in an instant. Boing! It was there - all of it. In describing the answer it must be noted that I then took the "packet" and translated it into meaningful words.

Most of you have had this happen. The information comes in with the mental, and emotional information, and sometimes actual pictures and feelings. You "know" the answer. This comes through your intuitive channels in a millisecond. Think on a specific incident in which this happened to you.

So, you might ask, why does a blunt-ended nail not spit the wood? Because it pushes through the wood rather than spreading it apart. I got a picture and a sense of what it meant.

Perspective is a tool in itself.

Here are a couple of "perspective" ideas that can be of value in understanding why and how things work with people, including, of course, you.

The first is:

> The World is a mirror.

Everything is connected. This is your reality. You have brought the person/situation to yourself because whatever part the other person is playing out, it has the same vibration as you at the moment. Thus what you see or are reacting to in that other person is really all about you.

When you point a finger at someone else, note that there are three fingers pointing at you. Names and accusations you direct at others are really you displacing your attitude towards your own internal actions. You are telling yourself about yourself. Take note!!

This is a powerful way to allow yourself to be triggered for finding behavior patterns you don't like and a wonderful opportunity to address them. It requires that you be aware of yourself in the moment.

Another concept worthy of note is that you can, and often do, have conflicting beliefs about a subject. Such as: "I believe this stuff works", and "I also believe that this stuff doesn't work."

I would like to share a personal experience along these lines. As a child I had rheumatic fever. Mother's remedies did not work and it took penicillin to eliminate the infection. As I grew up, I became interested in alternative medicines and used them extensively. While I believed alternative medicines did work sometimes (which is true), I also believed that they did not work, and "real" medicine was the only remedy for "important" diseases. Finding this belief, I used the "Circle of Experience" to eliminate the absoluteness of "alternative medicines don't work for 'real' diseases".

Do "real" medicines always work? No. Do alternative medicines always work? No. However, I allow that the perfect medicine will work and I will be led to it by the Universe because that is what I want.

Here we have another "tool". It is a tool of perspective. One of which you all are familiar. It is:

> You don't have to prove
> what you know is true.

This rule of life indicates that there is a hidden belief that is worth addressing. This will be much more apparent in others than it is in yourself, but once you start seeing it, you will begin to wonder if it applies to you in some regard. Remember: "The World is a Mirror".

You have all seen the show off, the social climber, and the person who must constantly tell you how wonderful they are and take every opportunity to let you know it. You have also seen those who are brilliant at or in something and never say a word. Their capabilities and accomplishments say it all.

Those who are driven to show you their wonderfulness don't believe a word of it. They are compensating for their true non-conscious belief that is that they have, and are, nothing. The situation here is that the conscious and the non-conscious are not in harmony. The strength of the non-conscious thought - that one is really faking it - is by far the more powerful energy-creator because the result is a fear-based belief that someone will find out the "terrible" truth - that you really have no value and you will be cast out.

Big safety issue!

It is important to remember that the person's own view of themselves has nothing to do with your view of them. In addition, if it is you that is seeming to be a "fake" (or whatever the label is), realize that this may well not be a conscious belief, but is non-conscious and needs to be let go using the "Circle of Experience".

The catch in these situations is that eventually -

> You WILL prove what you believe
> is your real truth.

Eventually those who are trying to prove what they know is not true will have to prove their "real truth" - which is the exact opposite of what they are showing on the surface. Sometime, somewhere, the screen will fall and disaster will strike in the form of the "real truth" sticking up its ugly head.

An example:

Three times in my life I have gotten into positions where I gave everything I had to prove I was lovable. Financial, emotional, time-wise, all of it, totally. Each time the situation ended in disaster where my "real" truth was proven which was that I believed that I was unlovable. In each case the person ended up hating me and driving me away, resulting in my being totally bewildered as to what had just happened.

It wasn't until the third situation, which was the most intense (and I had gained some insight into how things work), that I finally asked myself "What's going on here? What am I trying to prove that I know/believe isn't true?" As is often the case, once you perceive that something is going on and ask, you will get the answer right off. So then what?

I went to break the Circle of Experience. I know the source of this belief, for it is deep and echoes through time, but the truth is obvious for myself and all of Creation, and that is that we are all lovable -

Now.... <u>As we are</u>.

We will go into this in greater depth a little later.

Once you have eliminated your own beliefs concerning your non-lovability and love yourself unconditionally, then, if someone does not love you, it is because they cannot see the love that they are in you as a mirror to their beingness. It in no way says that you are not lovable.

There is a point to share that is sometimes difficult to understand but it is VERY important. It is this:

The human never does anything
it doesn't want to do
<u>at some level.</u>

What this means is that even if it doesn't make any sense that what you are doing you "want" to do, that is indeed the case. This comes from some level of which you are not aware. That level is non-conscious and you need to pursue why you are acting this way so you can eliminate the behaviors and resulting actions. You may say: " I hate my job. How can you say I "want" to stay here?" Well somewhere in your psyche you do.

Is it for:

The pain?
The suffering?
Because it is "safe" - a known quantity?
Because you are afraid of changing?
Because you are "trapped"?
Because you have "obligations"?
Because you can't find another job?
Because? Because? Because?

Find out the real reason and ask yourself if this is REALLY true or are you just responding to your programming and it is not NECESSARILY true.

How do you do this?

You have been introduced to the applied kinesiological approach for using your fingers to get a "strong" (yes) or "weak" (no) reaction to the use of a physical substance as well as the pendulum. These systems can also be used to ask yourself questions. Your intent as to what either system is used for will set the stage for your ability to ask whatever question you have.

Here is an example of how it can be used in a searching for the answer to a question in which you want to know what is REALLY going on. This example involves a reaction I had to a specific situation in which I couldn't figure out why I had such a strong emotional reaction. The technique can be used for any question.

The event to be processed can be either internally or externally stimulated. The reason behind the emotional response is what we're after. Let's take a specific situation based on a true story and see what's going on.

The story involves a man who was the owner of a convention center in which the President was speaking. He was complaining bitterly to a reporter on the air about how the President's programs have done nothing to help the job market. The reporter, having done his homework, asked if he, the owner, had not received "stimulus package" money to repair his center and thus provide jobs. The owner said "Yes". The reporter asked what did he do with the money. The owner replied he paid off the mortgage.

First state the reaction you just had.

I just had a strong emotional reaction to that situation. It made me very angry.

Statement: That situation made me extremely angry. (This confirms the situation and sets the tenor for the potential release.)

Q. Do I know what that was about?

Using the resisting finger method or pendulum;

A. Yes.

After asking each question that follows, use the technique. Don't forget to use the word "resist", if using kinesiology, before getting the answer.

Q. Was it the dishonesty of the owner in misusing the funds?

A: No.

Q: Was it stupidity of the owner in not realizing what he was saying?

A: No.

Q: Was it that the owner was attacking the President?

A: No.

Q: Well then what was it? Are we sure we know what made us angry?

A: Yes.

Keep pursuing the answer. It is there and it is you, not someone else.

You to yourself: Bring more to mind, then:

Q: Was it the ignorance shown?

"Ignorance" is a different word than "stupid" and will have different, though subtle, meanings to your non-conscious mind.

A: No.

Think for a bit, it will come.

Q: Was it arrogance?

A: No.

Q: Was it that the owner was a "fake" and trying to appear smart?

A: No.

Q: Was the owner being just plain "dumb"?

(Again, a subtle difference)

A: No.

Q: Was it the pushiness of the reporter?

A: No.

Q: Was it that the owner was "slow"?

A: No.

You: Good Grief! Are you SURE we know the answer?

A: Yes.

Think, think, THINK!.

Q: Is it the owner's closed-mindedness?

A: Yes.

What will most likely occur here is an "ah-ha" moment. It may not be wildly powerful, but the feeling is that you've "got it". What also will come is the reasoning behind the behavior pattern which, in this case, may be that the owner had a fixed idea about the President and there was no way anything could change his mind.

What I was telling myself through this exercise was that I believed I was closed-minded. It was a "truth" I did not want to hear, thus the emotional reaction. What did I do about it?

I asked myself if I am terminally "closed minded", and the answer was "no". Am I "closed minded" about some things?

The answer is "yes". And "SO WHAT !", it is part of how I have manifested and I love me as I am.

However, at a conscious level, I would rather be "open minded", so I can now be aware when something comes up and there is an automatic "knee-jerk" reaction. Such inflexibility is not a behavior that I wish to manifest. Thus I can allow for change in the "perfect me."

Notice that all the "reasons" I came up with for my reaction were about me and my internal beliefs and behavior patterns. No one has the answers except you and your own experienced-based psychology.

There is a true story that elegantly shows the power of a closed mind. It is possible you have experienced such behavior at one time or another. The person involved completely believed what she said and could not change, even in the face of overpowering (left brain) logic. The story is true.

A person walks into a coffee shop, sits down at the counter and orders a cup of coffee. The waitress asks what size and shows them two different sized cups. While doing this, she says, "It really doesn't make any difference, they are the same size." The customer sees that this is not true and decides to prove her wrong. The customer says "No they're not". She says "Yes they are." So he says, "Fill up that one with water (the larger one) and give me the other cup empty." She does and he proceeds to fill the smaller one to the brim, leaving water in the larger cup. The customer says, "See? This one is larger, there is still water in the other cup. " She says, "No it's not, they're the same size." He then proceeds to empty the remainder of the water into the smaller cup that then overflows onto the counter and onto the floor. Again, the customer says, "See?" She says, "Doesn't make any difference, they are the same size".

How many times have you lead someone step by step towards what you intend to be a logical conclusion, only to find the last step can not be taken, and the person reverts to their illogical, irrational belief? Simply put, people will believe what makes them safe in some critical way and the "logic" with which we are used to operating completely falls apart. There is a threat to them in accepting the "different approach" your "logic" offers, and it cannot be accepted. The new idea is totally unsafe and life-threatening.

We perceive ourselves as primarily logical beings but it is quite the opposite. We have a very thin veneer of logic over the "real" operating system - emotions. As mentioned before, and contrary to popular belief, we humans predominantly make our decisions emotionally, then use the left brain to justify our positions.

Once again, working with the beliefs does not require that you know the source of the belief, however, there are many times the source will come to mind when the belief is addressed. Personally, I find this of interest just because of the way I function (it's very male). A little later we go into looking into the sources of some of these beliefs.

There is another true story I would like to share at this point. Geese mate for life. The lady goose is the "leader" of the family and the male hangs around, as males seem to do. A friend had geese in her yard and one of the lady geese became her "pet". One day the lady goose followed the friend into the house. The man goose, trying to be brave, followed his mate into the house. Well it didn't take long for the male to become very nervous and he finally let go of goose-stuff on the floor and left the house in a most nervous condition. He was trying to be brave and overcome the natural fears that presented themselves around the new environment and people. He just couldn't contain himself under the stressful condition.

I share this for the following reason. Overcoming the "natural" fears we have, regardless of the source, can have a similar reaction for us. Not that we will "lose it" all over the rug, but that while we understand the illogical nature of our fear, we are still afraid and while trying desperately to be brave, remain afraid. This perspective may help you to understand why it is so difficult to just let the fears go. They are firmly fixed in the reptilian brain as survival issues and are too deep to "simply" go away. Tools given here can assist in addressing such fears and indeed letting them go. It takes conscious involvement in changing your reality.

How do you find these? For me, it is an emotional reaction to some incident that will trigger the reaction and then the search. Note that the convention center incident concerned an emotionally charged reaction. It was not centered in a belief, but in an automatic "learned" behavior pattern. The same technique is used for searching out and releasing unwanted beliefs.

Still another "trigger" potentially providing release of limiting programming concerns specific events that keep coming to mind from the past. Ask yourself what incidents of childhood or adulthood keep coming to mind with a dreaded feeling each time you think of it. Childhood memories of specific events or circumstances where you were "hurt" by others are good candidates. Losing your life savings in some situation or a loved one can also qualify, as can a serious injury that has current, permanent results. You might think of them every day or often, and at the slightest stimuli, they will pop into your conscious mind.

The question is what can you do to release the powerful emotional response? Often it requires therapy to release such programming, however, there is a technique that may help you to do some or all of the work yourself.

It must be noted here that if the reactions to these events are beyond your capability to look at them, work with a trained therapist is strongly recommended. Less severe events should be worked with at first to decide for yourself whether this technique will work for you.

In harmony with this desire to release limiting programming, another and very powerful "tool" is presented. The concept is a modification of the EMDR (Eye Movement Desensitization and Reprocessing) technique that involves eye movement to change internal reactions surrounding a specific event. In this technique no eye movement is required. Give it a try. It has been very successful with a number of those with whom I have worked. In some cases involving Post Traumatic Stress Syndrome, this technique has assisted in reducing the effects.

Again. If the event is too disturbing, see a qualified therapist!

The De-energizing Technique

We need an example, so I shall share one experienced with a woman who had a difficult relationship with her mother as a child. What came to her mind often was a picture in which she was in her bed watching through a window as her mother was leaving the house. She was inconsolable. Mother, who had a drinking problem and had been drinking, heard her wailing, came back in and hit her to make her shut up. Mother then left. The result was an intense feeling of being abandoned and of having no value. The participant remembered the incident vividly, as if it were yesterday.

The de-energizing technique involves looking at two sides of the situation.

First is identifying the emotional intensity of the experience on a scale of one to ten (ten being the highest). For the woman, it was obviously a ten.

Next is looking at the situation in perspective and rating the validity of the perspective on a scale of one to seven (seven being the highest in terms of believing that the perspective which is brought to the situation is valid).

What is the potential perspective to be brought to this situation? There are many points and I shall give a few. (Usually the participant comes up with additional personal ideas that make sense to them.)

- Mother was an alcoholic and did not have control of what she was doing.
- Mother did love her as a child but in her own way (not obvious to the child at that time).
- Mother had her own programming concerning both the drinking and the way she treated a child, probably based on her experiences as a child.
- Mother was doing the best she could with what she had and what she had was "stuff" - experiences that ended up with her responding to her programming at the time.
- This was a pivotal point in the child's life as she ended up with seemingly "harmful" programming. BUT, she would not be the person she is today if this event hadn't "shaped" her.

Ask what number, on a scale of 1-7, of these perspective items "feels" right. It should be a 7. You then go back to the energizing incident and ask yourself what is the level of emotional intensity now when you think about it. If the technique is working, the level will have reduced to a lower number.

If this number is still above a 4 or 5, go back to the "perspective side" and ask what additional perspective can be brought to the situation.

For the woman, the energy of the incident was still a 5, so we worked together to bring up some more "perspective items".

- The daughter was only 3 and had no way of knowing what was going on. Her physiological capabilities were just beginning to be developed.
- At that age, there was no other reaction she could have had.
- At that age she was indeed doing the best she could with what she had and her reaction was normal for a 3-year-old girl.
- Mother could have been having a really bad day for many other reasons - which the child didn't and couldn't have known.
- And, of course, mother did not abandon her. She did indeed return.
- It might also be that the girl could accept that she participated in the creation of this incident with her mother at some level so that she could learn a valuable life lesson.

What could the "lesson" be? Perhaps compassion for mother in her inability to move beyond her behaviors or addiction?

Compassion for her self as she realized what it was like to be "abandoned" so that she won't do the same to her children or others?

There are many possibilities, only limited by what comes to one's mind as a perspective on the situation.

After these additional points of perspective, with which the woman agreed are a 7, then she went back to the initiating situation and again was asked what is the emotional-response number. It went down to a 2 or 3. This was an acceptable number for the woman.

When one gets to a number with which you are comfortable, you have done the work on this issue. It may be zero or not. One's comfort with the number is what counts.

Being able to "re-live" the initiating situation without a big emotional rise is the goal.

The fear of being abandoned is inherent in the survival instincts of humans. This is a deep-seated response and can be triggered by many stimuli. One is the "disappearance" of mother when she goes out of sight from you as a baby. At the earliest stages of awareness, the baby lives in the absolute present and has no "experience" with time.

Another may be the family leaving you alone for any one of a number of reasons when you are growing up, loss of a lover or partner or child (yes we still feel abandoned), loss of friends (even though there are "logical" reasons), and abandonment of God in either this life or others when you are under great stress and "He" is silent.

This issue can also be dealt with using the de-energizing technique where part of the perspective is that you also participated in the choice of what is happening or happened, and the Universe is only doing what (at another level) you programmed for yourself. It is giving you what you asked for and now you are complaining. Hmmphhh.

Let's go back to beliefs.

Honesty is very important. This was mentioned before but keep in mind that although you may well consciously believe or not believe in something, the limiting belief may still be present and if not removed, it's vibration will continue to limit you in whatever you are pursuing. It is imperative that you allow that perhaps you do still have some residual belief in place so you can break the circle of experience and let it go.

Sometimes it is worthwhile to investigate both sides of the question. Do I believe that? And, do I also _not_ believe that?

Awareness is a key ingredient. Although this is a good idea all the time, watching yourself for Freudian slips, what song you are singing, some action (nodding "no" while saying "yes"), saying things that you really didn't intend to say ("It just came out") and most importantly, internal dialogue, especially judgments about anything that may come up. Have you ever tried to go 10 minutes without making a statement or having a thought that was not based on judgment? If you really want to try a hard exercise, try that one.

Back to "What do I believe that I had THAT ! reaction.?"

Your emotional reaction was caused by some stimulus. The external stimulus triggered a cascade of internal events that lead to some area of the brain that said: "I don't like that." Usually what you "don't like" is a reflection of yourself. The "mirror" of the world is showing you something that angers you about yourself. Your reaction is the same as if someone was calling you names or insulting you directly. Through this mechanism you are given an insight to some set of beliefs that you still harbor internally. Time to let them go. How? Through breaking the circle of experience.

Here are some of the possibilities that might have raised your emotional level:

I am stupid, slow, lazy, a bad person, inadequate, of no value and on and on. Most of the statements will be of a nature where you are judging yourself in some way.

All judgment comes from ignorance.

As a child we were ignorant for many reasons, among which is that our physiology was incapable of the same level of reasoning and understanding that we now have. Another reason for our ignorance is that we simply did not have the learning experiences, or our learning was limited by the source, or lack thereof.

Pick a philosophical point that interests you and look back at how you felt about it ten years ago. The basics may not have changed (or may have), but for sure the depth and additional information you have about it is greater than then. Learning is an unfolding process. Let it unfold.

Remember this:

There is no Shame in Ignorance.

And:
Shame, guilt, shoulda/coulda/woulda and so many of our reactions to life are no more than thinly disguised judgments on ourselves as is any self-deprecating statement.

When having an emotional response, you might ask yourself if it comes from one of these programmed behavioral responses:

Ignorance
Arrogance
Ego
Know-it-all
Existing "knowings"
Past actions that no longer pertain
Powerlessness
Having condemned oneself for something
Accepting condemnation (judgment) from outside yourself
Needing external validation for your "value".

There are obviously many more possibilities, only limited by your own programming and experiences.

Another tool that can be very useful is also based on perspective.

It assumes that you like and preferably love yourself as you are. Let's take the word "stupid". You have just called yourself "stupid" for some reason. Do this:

First ask yourself if everything you do is stupid? Are there no exceptions? Are you terminally stupid? The answer will be no. At least ONCE in your life you have done something intelligent. Come on, be honest. You are not terminally stupid or you wouldn't be reading this!

Next, say to yourself "Yes, I am sometimes stupid, however, it is a trait which is part of what I am - <u>and I like me</u> - and SO WHAT!" Sometimes it pays to be "stupid", so I shall keep that ability and call upon it <u>consciously</u> when it is useful.

You will have many of these and every one, at one time or another, will actually have value. Sometimes being stupid has value! So having the capability is a good thing. This is true of all those names you call yourself. Remember you are changing and that desire comes from being the person in this moment - with all the "flaws" which go to make you YOU. If someone else doesn't like you as you are, then tuff!

What we have done here is eliminate the REQUIREMENT to behave a certain way and replaced it with a choice!

This obviously is true for everyone, so give them a break too.

The next area we are going to address is central in changing your vibration. It concerns self-worth.

We have mentioned this before but it is time to go into the background of why our self-image/self worth is generally poor and what we can do about changing that. Ideas and exercises are "tools" presented here so you can change your vibration to one of self-love. Unconditional love of your self at all levels is the goal.

What does "unconditional" mean? It means that there are NO conditions that will diminish your love of yourself as you are. A mother does not have "conditions" under which she loves her child, no matter how "bad" their behavior is.

Be the "mother" of yourself!

A poor self-image is inherent in the human condition. It is a necessary component to the learning we do from the beginning. It all starts with the concept of "good" and "bad". As an infant we learn to respond in certain ways to get what we want. "Good" actions get "good" results and "bad" actions get correspondingly "bad" results. We grow and learn in this mode and therefore have that part of us is "bad" as part of our outlook on life. This "duality " is inherent in the human experience.

The first element in changing this is perspective. We were (and are) not "good" or "bad" children. We were just children. Learning and growing is part of the human condition. This has been true for all our lives and remains a basic "truth" of our beingness. We are all experiencing life and making decisions from those experiences and doing the best we can with what we have. What we have, as mentioned earlier, is programming (stuff). Everyone has programming. Can't not.

Inherent in this concept is the release of judgment against yourself for being who, what, where, how and why you are, and having done whatever you did to get here now. Where you are now is Perfect in the unfoldment of your individual self AND the unfoldment of the Universe.

YOU ARE NOT YOUR BEHAVIOR PATTERNS

In the process of judging everything and trying to find who we were and are, there has always seemed to be a significant element of confusion. A good reason for this is that we have identified with our behavior patterns, our job, family or some external manifestation of our environment. Another reason for confusion is that our behavior patterns have changed over time. Add to this that they change during the day, depending on the circumstances, and confusion is the only possible result.

Change Your Reality

At work you manifest one set of behaviors, when singing in the shower another, at church another and when courting another, and on and on. You literally have thousands of behavior patterns and draw on them as serves the purpose of the moment. As long as you identify with what you do and how you do it, you are not going to be able to come to an acceptable conclusion about "who" you are. Once again, this is offered :

>You are the Energy of the Universe (Love)
>manifest as a point of consciousness
>in the present.
>Everything else is what you do.

A thought:

>The most powerful thing you can do
>is to BE the love that you are.

Within the competitive environment we have set up for ourselves, trying to be as good as, or better than our internal expectations or anyone else's, we naturally instill judgmental programming and draw on it continuously. Just listen to yourself during any day and watch how many times you might say:

"That was stupid."
"I am really slow."
"I am very stubborn".
"I am a slow learner."
"I am really lazy."
"I have no value."
"I just don't have it."

and, of course:

"I don't deserve it."
because "I am a bad person."
and, and, " And............"

When any programmed responses of this nature come up, the first step you take with it is to break the circle of experience.

It is necessary to identify the specific "name" you are calling yourself to bring it into perspective. You break the "Circle of Experience" and then do the "SO WHAT" exercise and allow that it is all a part of how you are manifesting. You are <u>more</u> than OK!

Say again how you like you, your "manifestation".

- a lot
- as you are
NOW.

Recalling the "mirror" that the world presents to you, you now know that when you point the finger at someone or something and call it a name, you are really pointing the other three fingers at yourself and it is you that doesn't like your own preprogrammed responses to the world. The release of this programming is first to ask yourself if you do indeed have this "trait" all the time.

Well, are you, or do you? "No" is the answer. Even if it (whatever "it" is) is sometimes or often true, it is not ALWAYS true. So. "NO" is the answer.

Next you ask yourself if sometimes you are. The answer is "Yes". However, that trait is part of who and what you are, and you like you as you are and: "SO WHAT!!"

Would you like to be more open-minded or different? Sure, but that is a choice that depends on circumstances. Now that you are more aware, you can use the capability when you think it is appropriate and not use it when you choose.

In the case of "closed minded", for instance, the pattern is a defensive, fear-based reaction which says that one is afraid of being able to handle "new" information/situations/perspectives. And that the certainty in what one knows makes one feel "safe". This means, of course, that one feels unsafe with change.

Self judgment, on the order of "bad" is part of the polarity/duality condition we all live with, and humans have chosen to label each side of the duality with terms such as "good" and "bad", but The Universe has no such concept.

It's All Just Experience.

A thought:

> There is not a single moment of your existence
> that has not been
> Perfection
> on your chosen path of evolvement.

It is natural on the part of an intelligent person to create high expectations of their behavior beginning as a young child. The problem is that these "expectations" are generally way beyond our ability to perform, thus setting up a failure modality that will persist for a lifetime. The powers of Superman, Batman and all the heroes combined are never powerful enough for a child. "Never enough" is the operating system. Thus "failure" is in the cards for most endeavors.

> Never Enough
> is a fiction.

We may tend to fear we will be punished or abandoned if we do not fulfill what we believe to be the expectations of us by ourselves or others. This is a deeply set human reaction based on the "genetically-driven truth" that if we are abandoned in the very early years, we will indeed die.

The "rub" is that we are always doing the best we can with what we have, and the built-in mechanisms of "never enough" dominate and keep us in a strong negative self-judgment posture for a lifetime. We never seem to be able to achieve our own expectations and judge ourselves without mercy.

Within religious philosophies, whatever requirement is placed before us, the child-mind sees it as impossible to achieve, resulting in potential confirmation that we are "unworthy". This "unworthiness" can lead to fear of punishment or abandonment or at the least, being cast out.

As mentioned before, what we all have is "stuff", the programming of lifetimes, and although we like to think we can control what we do, seldom is it an easy task. This is due to the imbedded programming of the past being deeply set within the 20 million bits of non-consciousness that really runs our lives. The tools to change that programming and change our vibration and thereby change our lives is the work of Changing Your Reality.

As mentioned before, the goal is to bring your conscious and non-conscious minds into harmony. Here are some ideas to think about and some exercises to do to help you work on this.

The background: The internal relationship we have had with ourselves, especially those who are intelligent, is often a sado-masochistic one in which part of us is constantly finding fault with what we are doing or have just done. We are merciless in judging ourselves as not having done well enough no matter how well others say they think we have performed. In short we have always viewed ourselves internally as failures and a fake. This constant requiring of us to be better than we are has as its basis wanting to belong and be accepted by someone or some group in order to (from a genetic place) keep us safe.

Change Your Reality

We have come to accept this internal relationship as the way it is and are loathe to change it because it would seem to mean that we are rejecting the other part of self as it currently exists. This potential rejection is one of the most frightening possibilities the internal self can imagine. It is thus totally unacceptable.

Until:

We come to realize that the S&M modality is not the real basis for our internal relationship that we think it is. What we really cherish is the close buddy relationship we have with ourselves. We have come to depend on that "other" self to always be there and always support us in what we do - in all ways and always. Underneath the surface behaviors is the best buddy we have ever had, and we want to keep it that way - familiar and comfortable.

The real basis for wanting to maintain both of ourselves in tact is the total love that we deeply feel for that "other" part of our self and the total feeling of safety its presence brings us. This works in both directions. So the antagonistic surface behavior patterns become unnecessary as we come to know their source and what it is we really desire. "Losing" that "best friend" is, in itself, not a happy thought. The idea is to integrate you "both" into a wondrous single you, loving YOU.

There is a significant point here that is worthy of note:

The love of a child is conditional.

It is conditional upon it receiving what it wants. These wants are driven by the genetic need to survive. Only later do we learn what unconditional love is. A mother knows this from the moment of a child's birth. There are no "conditions" upon the love. The child can "misbehave" and there is no diminishing of that love. There may be anger, frustration and annoyance, but the underlying love continues. While this may seem idyllic, you have the idea, and, it is totally possible! The internal dialogue with yourself concerning the conditional love of "your best buddyrole" is that you love yourself totally <u>as you are,</u> and there is no further requirement that you beat yourself up or be beaten up in order to be safe. You need to convince yourself - both child and adult - that you have the safety of your unconditional love for all that you were and are.

Bringing the child and the adult into synergy is accomplished by making the child feel safe in your (the adult's) hands. First you have to feel safe. That's the desired result of this work.

Feelings are the real driving force in creating our reality. We seek not the events, but the feelings associated with those events that lead us to the other item that creates our reality:

We live to serve our feelings.

Feelings often create the beliefs that we serve. We feel terrible as a result of some event and come to believe that that event is "bad", as is any event that is even slightly similar. We will literally do anything to avoid that feeling again. In a similar manner, those events that have produced "good" feelings will be pursued in order to repeat the high. This may lead to obsessive behavior where the high must be obtained and exceeded by additional highs. The latter is called addiction.

If some event in your life (loss of a loved one, loss of a job, loss of your home or nest egg or any traumatic event) has resulted in a "sinking feeling" (if it has happened, you know what that is), you will do anything to avoid that feeling again. You will avoid falling in love again because the last love lost was so traumatic you can't bear (emotionally and thus programming-wise) to have it happen again. Therefore you will not let yourself fall in love again and if you do you it will take a very long time to "let go" and love at that total level of involvement. This is

Change Your Reality

why the first time you fall in love is so intense (no limits) and ever after you have a "better prospective" which really means no one will get in so deep ever again. It is a defense mechanism that limits our experiences in this case and any other where that "sinking feeling" has occurred.

We humans naturally create a duality within ourselves as a check and balance for deciding what to do. For each person the internal relationship this creates lasts for a lifetime, seldom changing in dynamics unless we consciously pursue a change. For some, it is an antagonistic relationship that no longer serves our purpose in pursuing safety and happiness. This CAN be changed. It calls for a new perspective.

Here is an exercise to help in this change.

Imagine that you are some young age (5?, 8?, 11?). Think of yourself as being with yourself being the same age. The two of you are standing next to one another in some safe place. Allow yourself to feel the comfort, love and safety of knowing that next to you is your best buddy. <u>Acknowledge</u> that this is the person you depend on for everything and without whom you cannot imagine existing. Let the feeling of warmth and fuzziness totally engulf you as you turn to you other self and give him/her the warmest most wonderful hug you can imagine. HOLD IT. Think that no matter what this other person did or does or would do or can do, it will never make any difference in how you feel about them.

That is unconditional love and THAT is what we really seek in all the theatrics of behaviors we think we have to perform to get what we really want. That love is unconditional. And it makes us feel <u>safe</u>. It is present all the time and always has been. Because we think of ourselves as omnipotent when we are children, we think another loves us only because we have done something. So we do it again and again to achieve what we desire. BUT, like mother's love, it was always there regardless of our antics. The behaviors are just theatrics generated from ignorance resulting from the natural human condition.

To expand a bit concerning the nature of love, it should be noted that for most, love is a <u>learned</u> response. What this means is that love, as we grow up, is most often conditional. You do this and you get that. That is "love". You behave and mother gives you a cookie. That is love. What the "condition" part of "conditional" is, is the expected feeling of safety that you get from getting what you want and knowing that you have "pleased" your parent. The unconditional capability only comes later and is often in considerable conflict with what we have learned love is. Many relationships are beleaguered by this problem.

An important extension of this concept is that whatever a child experiences in their growing up is what "love" or a "loving atmosphere" is to them. An example is an abusive or alcoholic relationship in the family, where what a child learns and therefore seeks as it grows is a recreation of that "loving" relationship. This is why so many abused children end up in abusive relationships. Realizing this can significantly assist in removing that expectation and related behavior patterns so you can indeed have a relationship centered in unconditional love. Both the "circle of experience" and the "de-energizing technique" are tools that will help you change this condition.

Have you ever felt unconditional love? Not from someone, but within yourself towards someone or something else? Certainly if you have children you have, especially if you are the mother. For a father this is also totally possible. When you fell in love with another for the first time, did you not feel the "feeling" that no matter what they did you would love them always? Well, maybe "always" didn't occur, but the moment was real. Having a pet can bring forth that feeling, so can loving nature in any of its aspects. There are a myriad of potential experiences where love without condition can be experienced.

Change Your Reality

This feeling is not generally the purview of a child. He/she is too involved with doing what is necessary to survive.

I would like to share some quotes from Ken Carey's book *Starseed, The Third Millennium*:

"You do not have the capacity to fail. Failure is the illusion of those who dwell continuously upon errors. Those who are afraid to make mistakes serve a god of fear."

And there is another:

"There are no arbitrary standards of perfection."

This has been quoted from Ken Carey earlier in the book, however, it is worth reading again.

"To live spontaneously, instinctually. To simply be. To say the right words without thinking them out ahead of time. To experience the purity of a mind uncluttered by troublesome and misplaced responsibility. To know exactly the right gesture, the right behavior, the creative responses for each and every situation. Such are the birthrights of each and every human being."

What we are doing in this work is resetting your existing paradigm on two fronts. One is that you create your reality and are not a victim. Two is that you are incomparable within the Universal All and have value for the unique experiences you bring to the Consciousness of Being. Some say ceasing to judge your self is the final step to enlightenment. You will cease to judge others and situations long before this last step. Others have said that the "final judgment" is the last time you judge yourself.

We are all in this together and separately. Honoring someone else's path honors you on yours - the same for respecting. Remember, the world is a mirror.

Being on the path of awareness, you will note that the Universe will bring to you little hints, wisps of ideas that sail through your mind, and events which may seem to be unrelated to what you desire, but on closer inspection are worth drawing into your greater awareness and perspective.

If you can be aware of these "wisps" and grab onto them, you can gain some additional insights that may be of value.

As mentioned earlier, the most prevalent limiting condition we have is that of a poor self-image. This stems from our experiences and the reactions we have to them in trying to validate our worth. Two factors play out here, the first being the genetically-driven need to survive and continue to be accepted by the group. The second being the judgment of ourselves as not meeting some internally-created expectation regarding our response to external events.

As children we seek validation of our worth from our parents, family, teachers, peers and anyone else who will tell us we have value. It is a good guess that if you are reading this, the validation necessary to make you feel a considerable sense of worth was, to a significant degree, missing. In this situation the child, fearing that they will be rejected, "discarded", and abandoned will try anything, including what might appear to be "bad" behavior to obtain the attention and validation of its worth. ANYTHING to be acknowledged!! ANYTHING to not be abandoned or discarded. Your survival is at risk!

If you keep in mind that what you seek here is really the unconditional love of your mother and had it, <u>regardless of what you did</u>, then you can let much of the self-worth antics go. It was simply you playing out the omnipotent nature of believing that you caused everything and therefore needed to continue these behaviors to get what, in fact, you already had.

Exercise:

Change Your Reality

This exercise assumes that you had a close relationship with your mother at least for the first few weeks after birth.

Imagine being an infant and resting at your mother's chest. She is holding you and breathing softly. There are just the two of you and the environment is quiet and sweet. Imagine the feeling of warmth and closeness. Imagine the feeling of total safety. Not a worry in the world. Just the love. If you can feel this, you are feeling the unconditional love she had for you as a child. If you can recall this feeling, as in the exercise with yourself, you know the real feeling you sought/seek. Can you feel that way about yourself? All self-judgment has to go away to truly move on.

The antics are no longer necessary because you can feel the true unconditional love that you seek. It never was necessary to work for it and it isn't now. You have it permanently in your conscious mind. When you find yourself doing some behavioral antic just to get attention and that feeling of love, you can stop and tell yourself you don't need to do that any more because you do love yourself, as you are now. You already have it and let the old energy go. There IS a choice.

Remember that it is the feelings we seek and any stimulus that creates that feeling is acceptable. In the case of mother's unconditional love, the hugging of your self or your pet can have the same wonderful effect. So, potentially can looking in the mirror and telling yourself "I Love You". In these cases it is you that is feeling the unconditional love. This latter stimulus is available now, whereas mother's love may only be a memory.

A bit of perspective is necessary to be honest during the next exercise. When we say "you have done and are doing the best you can with what you have", most will balk. The reason for this is that they will tell themselves they could have or should have done "better".

In addition, if we believe that ceasing to judge ourselves will let us off the hook of doing anything, and we would lose all incentive to accomplish anything - well, that's just not true. If you remember that most all of our responses are automatic, you will also accept that little thinking and much programming have almost always determined your response. You live your life on automatic by setting the starting point in events and letting your experience take you where you have gone before. As an exercise in perspective, think of a huge computer that has all of you and your experiences internally programmed in memory. You put in a stimulus and out would come a most probable response. For the most part, your reactions would be totally predictable by this machine. That's pretty much the way it works, so thinking you should have or could have done something different under most circumstances is illusory.

The next point is the one of the "Perfection" of circumstances and their outcome for everyone involved. This is TANA (There Are No Accidents). So, with that in our minds, here is:

Another exercise:

Imagine where you are right now there is a child next to you. It is you at some early impressionable age. Look over at them and feel their presence. How do you feel about them?

Can you feel compassion for the life you know they will have to live? What would you tell them? Would you reassure them that it will turn out all right? What advice would you give them? Actually tell them what you would say. Say the words.

Ask them to come and sit on your lap. Imagine holding them and loving them as much as you can and as much as ever they wanted. Tell them you will keep them safe and here is the proof: here you are and they've obviously made it this far.

Tell them how proud you are of them for having dealt with so much and kept their head about them. Praise them for their stick-to-it attitude. Let them know you understand fully what they are going through, even if no one else does. Tell them you will be their best friend forever. Tell them you love them so much that simple words just can't tell them how you really feel.

FEEL the truth of your thoughts and words and thank them for being who, what, when and how they were. Tell them you'll keep in touch and especially that you will keep them safe.

There is a point worth making here and it is a general difference between compassion and empathy. Empathy is being able to feel the same as someone else. Usually where there is suffering of some sort, the Empath will feel the negative effects along with the other person. The energies of the other can easily bring a person down. Compassion, on the other hand, is being able to relate to someone's situation but not "take on" their pain. Being in a compassion mode, rather than empathetic, you can be of considerably more help and service to both of you.

It is compassion you want to bring to yourself as the child, maintaining sufficient distance from the pain to stay in the most helpful mode. Setting intent puts your work with yourself in a left-brain position to guide you in the emotional healing.

Allow this to integrate with you for a while. Let the exercise stand alone before you proceed with this next one. Go do something else rather than continue to read. It is important to allow the rum to integrate with the cake.

There is a third exercise in this group. It is with you and you in the Now.

Go to a comfortable place where there is room enough for two and sit down. Relax for a moment and when you have achieved this, picture yourself sitting next to you. Actually turn your head towards your other self and tell yourself what you think of that person.

Do you like them?

Tell them what qualities you think they have.

Tell them what you think is wrong. Then tell them that you know they are doing the best they can under the circumstances and it's OK, you'll love them anyway. Tell them what they are doing right and be generous with praise.

Tell them that the "flaws" and "imperfections" they think they have aren't flaws at all, but different aspects of how they have manifested. Tell them that they are totally acceptable because these "flaws" come together and make them what they are right now - and that is very special.

Tell them that their worth is not dependent on words or deeds but on simply being the Love that they are. And that they ARE Love.

Tell them "what they are" is pretty wonderful - truly full of wonder.

Tell them that there isn't another person alive you would rather have take you through life.

Would you like to have them as your lover?

Now just look at them and see their Perfection. See how hard they have worked to do their best. Feel compassion for them on their path and know that there is a deep-seated love that you wish to express towards this person, your "other" self.

Close your eyes and imagine standing up and hugging yourself. Feel the love towards your self. Say the words: "I love you."

Dwell on this. Realize you are a very remarkable and magical person on a path leading to your happiness, and won't give up for even a moment.

Again, put this all down for a bit and let the work settle in.

This has ben mentioned before, but is worth sharing again:

Stand in front of a mirror and look yourself in the eyes. Say out loud "I Love You", and "we're doing just fine". Do this often.

You might also do a nightly review of the day and think of the things that made you happy. For some, keeping a journal serves as a reminder that we can indeed create happiness, but we must remain aware in order to validate our changes. Such ideas also raise your vibration. For some, "counting your blessing" may help falling asleep.

Take another break and let this experience settle in. Keep it up for as long as you wish, and do it any time you feel down on yourself. Be generous with your love towards yourself. Most of all - keep perspective.

Remember, smiling, even when you don't feel like it, changes your body chemistry positively - so do these exercises.

An exercise in compassion:

For just a moment, imagine that you are the person who decided to become the person you have become, and you knew what you were going to go through before you were born. You knew what the "setups" were before they even became reality. Now feel what it would be like to have set up a child (you) for such a difficult job. Feel the compassion you would have for "doing this" to any child, especially yourself. Say and feel that you are sorry, and that you would like that innocent child to forgive you for "doing this". Just feel the compassion and let yourself know that you love all of yourself unconditionally, and want "all of you" to work together as you deal with your future. Think of yourself as a cohesive "team" – Team You – that is going to face the new and wonderful future you are working towards. Together, as one.

A significant part of the work for the child to be accepted will be dealing with internal judgments which powerfully invalidate it's own worth in it's own eyes. These are the "antics" of which we speak and this becomes a habit pattern over time. The resulting self-deprecation results in an almost impossible condition to overcome. It is generally deeply hidden and denied in adulthood, so overcoming that self-deprecation can be a life's work. With the exercise and concepts above, you may find yourself no longer needing to play the S&M game because all you really wanted, and want, is the unconditional love of yourself, your buddyrole. Experience and feel that truth.

If you can feel that you never did anything "wrong" (from a cosmic, rather than a social perspective), but simply had experiences on your journey of awareness, then you don't need to forgive yourself because it all had purpose. At the same time it does not hurt to apologize to those you "wronged" as you say to yourself "I won't do that again". If you still need to forgive yourself, then do it.

Addiction to some of these behavior patterns is not unusual. While we originally "needed" and "depended" on them for survival, expression of these traits can become something on which we are still dependent, but no longer find fruitful. We seemingly can not give them up no matter how hard we try.

Some of the potential addictive emotional patterns can be:

Fear
Self-judgment
Blaming yourself for everything negative
Anger
Stress
Anxiety
Drama
Unhappiness
Misery
Illness
Pain
Suffering
Self-martyrdom
Poor me
Nastiness
Disappointing one self
Valueless
Worthlessness

Being nothing
Self destructiveness
Seeking terror
Seeking intense emotional experiences
Seeking punishment for being "bad"
Pressure to perform

And so many more. Add to your list as it applies.

Then there are the physical addictions that seldom exist without an emotional component. These include drugs, alcohol, smoking, eating disorders and many more.

Self-judgment is totally normal. The most brilliant person I know considered himself to be a fake because he always "could have done better". He knew the truth, and nothing anyone said would change that internal judgment.

So what do you do about these?

First, bring the awareness to consciousness that that behavior is indeed addictive for you. This can be done through simply being aware of yourself and your actions in the present, noting that you just can't let something go or stop acting in some manner.

Second, set your mind to change the situation and eliminate the "addictive" <u>component</u> of the behavior from your vibrational sphere.

Third, address the Universal computer with a command, saying "computer (Universal Oneness, God, whatever name you wish) I want the addiction to _____ removed from my vibrational sphere now. Make it so! And thanks." Be calm and determined in your statement, knowing that it is <u>done</u> as you speak.

What is intended to happen is that the addiction be removed. What is left is just the behavior pattern that can be dealt with using the tools in this chapter.

There are several thoughts that may be of value in gaining perspective, some of which are shared here. Some are simple statements, others are more complex ideas. They belong to the "facts" part of the "Hierarchy of Knowledge" given below, which is in itself an interesting approach to learning and action.

The Hierarchy of Knowledge

1. Facts: Facts are things you know to be true. Even knowing something is not true is a true fact in this instance. They may change with time and therefore affect your whole hierarchy. Facts are the result of a sorting of information on any subject you choose. This is usually done internally through your built-in filter. Most information is discarded and only that which supports your existing belief systems will be admitted.
2. Knowledge: This is the accumulation of facts over time. This continues until you die and therefore will change over time as well. There is a natural sorting of the facts and information collected which becomes the basis for this step. Both of these steps have filters that dictate what will be included in your developing philosophical concepts.
3. Understanding: This deals with interrelationships of the knowledge you have been collecting. It is the tie connecting all the facts and knowledge into a cohesive philosophical construct. Here too, a sorting is done in order to have a unified posture towards life.
4. Insight: here "new" ideas come to add to the construct of your philosophy.
5. Perspective: A greater context of understanding that brings ideas outside the specific subject being

considered and speaks of the relationship of all the things you know as a cohesive whole.
6. Wisdom: This is the work of integrating all the previous steps into action. While a wise person seems to know a lot and be very capable, it is their actions that show them to be "wise".
7. Enlightenment: The achievement of harmony with all aspects of your existence, physical and non-physical.

Note that as one proceeds through life, the natural sorting according to your existing philosophy creates a "box" (defined in Chapter 1) that usually precludes completely new ideas and paradigms, as well as locks us into existing ideas and actions. Most of us would like to think we think "outside the box" and are "open" to new ideas and change. However, to actually do this in regards to some subjects, the entire hierarchy may have to be modified. This is naturally "scary" to the ego - which is not generally comfortable in this "change" mode. The ego and its mechanics are discussed in the next chapter.

Often the object of our anger is not available to bring your energy into a comfortable balance. An example might be of a person who has died, or is not around, but for whom you hold negative reactions.

> You do not need the object of your
> anger to release it.

The following ideas can be hard to accept, but take any subject and think about it. Perspective is necessary.

The basis for judgment is ignorance.

> Where there is judgment,
> wisdom cannot reside.

Concerning perspective:

> The true measure of the clarity of awareness
> is the ability to maintain perspective.

Concerning expectations:

> If you have no expectations,
> you will never be disappointed.

Concerning trust:

> You cannot trust others until you trust
> your self.

Trust is one of the most difficult qualities to achieve; especially when you cannot identify that which you are trying to trust with your five senses. Working with the Universe raises this point very powerfully. So, the question is how many experiences does it take to trust that the Universe is indeed on your side and fulfilling your desires? The answer?

> How ever many it takes for you.
> It is totally personal.

In dealing with life's conditions, there are two ideas that may be of value:

> Question everything.

> Discernment.
> Always discernment.

Certainly fear is one of the major concerns with which we have to deal in this life. For most it is an important goal to move out of fear into the freedom of joy, happiness, love and peace. However, there are some thoughts on fear that may assist in understanding its nature and effect upon you.

1. Getting rid of all fears for most is unreasonable. It is the fears of imaginings and memories that might happen, but are not likely, that must be brought to perspective. We can imagine danger in all things if we want to. And we may want to. Conspiracy theorists do this very well. They are always the victim. Remember, the human animal never does anything it doesn't want to do at some level. The reason to get rid of fears is because it attracts to you the very things you fear.
2. Some perspectives of fear are:
Fear is a natural part of our being.
Fear is necessary for certain safety conditions.
Fear creates emotional blockages that are limiting.
Fear can be released.
All fears we wish to remove are program based.
Fear does not <u>usually</u> make you or keep you safe.
Fear overrides reason and too often - safe action.
Fear manifests through behavior patterns you don't like.
Fear can be an habitual response, even an addiction.
Fear and self-image are often interwoven.
You can feel fear. There is a bodily reaction.
Once fear is raised it will remain active for any given situation.
There is no automatic release of fear programming.
The ego is Always on watch.
The reptilian brain is Always ready to take action.

> The ego projects our experience-based fears into possible negative futures.
> Experiences are not guaranteed to repeat. The ego doesn't know that.
> Fears must be eliminated through reprogramming, ONE at a time.
> Fears can be carryovers from other lives.
> If you still fear, you have more programming that relates.

This point has been made before and is worthy to be made again:

Fear, as any aspect of your personality, goes to make up who you are now. Being afraid is OK. You love your self AS YOU ARE NOW! SO WHAT if you are afraid! You have chosen to change being controlled by fear, and that is the work. There is NOTHING wrong with you. NOTHING! You are a work in progress. Love yourself for the perseverance that keeps you going.

To move from fear to peace through perspective is one of the reasons we are on this planet.

In this regard, as just mentioned, one of the key perspectives is:

> The ego lives from the past into the future,
> not in the present.

Living in the moment removes most fears that are based on experiences and projected by the ego into the future to keep you safe.

One of the most annoying occurrences in this work is the re-emergence of some issue you think you have addressed and removed. An idea that can make this easier is to think of the spring on the back of a flashlight that looks like a Christmas tree. As it goes around and around it gets smaller until it reaches a point. Each time you come around again to what appears to be the same subject, you have in fact gotten to another level of the issue that needs to be addressed. However, this time you have additional learnings and perspective to be able to work with the issue. Eventually you will come to the point at the end of the spring that represents the end of having to deal with that particular issue, and the issue will be gone. Pursuit of the release of limiting energies is never a wasted effort.

Some of you might find that with everything going well, you get into a particularly happy place and then things seem to fall apart and more stuff comes up. This is because the feeling of happiness or bliss "awakes" the deeper fears associated with "dangerous" change. Simply go after the programming again and release it. Eventually your happiness will not bring forth new "negative" programming because there isn't any left.

A thought:

Life is a set of priorities. Where are yours?

Now, a point to ponder and accept. If you have decided to work towards your betterment, then the Universe will back you. No matter what you do;

YOU CAN NOT DO IT WRONG.

Think on this:

> You can not love
> that which is in the moment,
> unless you love
> everything that went to create it.

REMEMBER:

   REMEMBER:

      <u>REMEMBER</u>:

PERSPECTIVE

      Use it
        or
     lose it !

Chapter 5

THE EGO AND CONSCIOUSNESS

The ego is one of the most interesting aspects of our humanity. When looking into how we operate, our behavior patterns and our survival needs, the ego is where we want to focus our work. Perspective is definitely required to keep the ego's functions and reasons for actions in harmony with our desired goals of freedom and peace.

It is necessary to look at the source and various functions of the ego in order to be able to work with it to change our reality. It is also worthwhile to look at some examples of how the ego limits our freedom to change.

First off, the ego is NOT our enemy. It is our protector and friend and its functions are gifts to assist us in negotiating the world around us. The ego's primary function is to keep us safe. It works in concert with the reptilian brain and within a limiting physiological structure that exists from birth.

The ego has no intelligence. It is solely reactive from the basis of rules established by genetics and experience.

But there is more, MUCH more. I would like to share with you some thoughts about the nature of ego and spirit harmony from Ken Carey's book *Starseed, The Third Millennium*.

"Decision making (within the human body) was never intended to be dominated by the sensory input of the natural egoic process. While the spirit dispassionately reviews sensory input with the clear-sighted objectivity of eternal awareness, the ego, on the other hand, proceeds differently. Its way of utilizing and experiencing the branching, treelike human nervous system was unlike the spirit's. The ego feels the human nervous system subjectively, sensuously, slowly, and in detail, taking time to groom and care for the body and attend to its needs. Though different, the ego's and the spirit's respective uses of the human nervous system are both vital, both essential to a balanced incarnate experience. "

The spirit part of our system draws from the infinite awareness of all of reality and processes responses to situations at the speed of light, thus responding instantaneously with a broad-based answer. This is transmitted every time as the "first impulse", the first thought that comes to mind. It is called intuition. If you make a habit of listening to it, you will find that it will lead you to where you want to go.

The ego, on the other hand, will process the answer based on its limited experiences and is processed through the time-consuming interpretations and mechanics of the human nervous system.

Thus the balanced ideal within the functioning human is to combine both the intuitive and experiential bases for living a happy life.

"Spontaneity is a rational process in the constitution of love. Its accuracy is unsurpassed. It is not clouded by fear-rooted emotions, cultural bias, or addiction to linguistically structured thought". (*Starseed, the Third Millennium,* Ken Carey)

This provides another "tool" to begin to use and consciously develop. It is listening to the "first impulse", knowing that it is from the heart center. The "problem" with this is that even thinking that you are going to use the "first impulse", immediately turns on the mind. It has to "just happen" and requires being aware in the moment.

Some of the problems surrounding the ego evolve within the human as a result of the way it is formed and develops. From the first life experiences, the ego is highly active, standing guard for our survival as the higher-functioning portions of the brain develop. It triggers a fear response when danger is perceived. This can be hunger, having your diapers full, being "abandoned" when mother isn't seen and any unsafe condition it perceives. Its perception at this level is primitive but effective. As time passes and the brain develops, these triggers remain and are added to by "hurtful and dangerous" experiences that occur.

At the early stages of evolvement, those things that qualify as "hurtful and dangerous" are very broad and viewed from the black and white simplicity that a child inherently brings to early life. Discernment, requiring the higher levels of brain development, is not available at this stage.

As life progresses, experiences that "look like" these early "hurtful and dangerous" events are filtered through the simple logic of the early brain and branded as something to be avoided. Even when the developing mind thinks the new experience might be fun and safe, the reptilian brain, through the ego, will raise fears that will cause you to be cautious in giving it a try. Realizing that the fears may be unfounded, you have choice as to whether to continue or not. Often it is "not" because of the inherent power of the fear-based programming.

The human brain, being very large, has the capacity to remember everything and keeps those things that are unsafe in storage to be compared to any new experience. Thus none of the early broad-brush prohibited actions are eliminated "just in case" the situation may come up again. This leads to situations in later life wherein early behavior patterns, based on safety as perceived by the ego, become dysfunctional.

For the ego, the "flight, fight or freeze" responses are natural outcomes when any danger is perceived to be extreme.

The ego has several functions, the most important of which is the sense of individuality within our culture and indeed creation. It manifests in many ways. The necessity for individuality is genetically driven for the species to survive.

In the natural order of survival, group survival will dominate over the individual. Thus the driving forces behind the willingness to give one's life for some cause is an integral part of the ego's operational modality.

The earliest manifestation of the ego occurs very early in our development. It is the point at which the consciousness exerts its individuality through the power of "no". This is such an early age that the functioning of the brain is minimal and thus this programming ends up very deeply seated. "No" is the ultimate manifestation of power and individuality. The ego feels powerless because it comes from a place of having no power and belonging totally to mother. The result is that in using "no", the ego is working to prove what it knows is not true - that it is powerful and independent. Having to prove one is powerful and independent are traits that are natural and necessary in the development of the human psyche.

However, a very important problem arises within the child. While it is driven to be independent it also wants to remain in the safety of mother's arms. Through life this duality of both wanting and not wanting to be independent creates problems. While the ego will say "yes" to some requests to show its power and independence, it will also fear being alone. Being aware of this dichotomy can help in bringing behaviors into perspective and potentially achieving an acceptable balance.

Using the "Circle of Experience" can allow the triggered early emotional reactions to things that seem "ridiculous" now to be addressed and released. The key, once again, is the <u>emotional</u> reaction.

Normally the family unit provides the safety for the child to practice becoming independent. Our goal in this work is to bring to the ego a sense of BOTH comfort with its individuality and the promise of true safety in belonging as well as being in harmony with the rest of you. You are the new "safe" home.

Consciousness, both the 40 bit and the 20 million bit parts is a filter through which all experiences are "tested" for being safe. If these incoming experiences are perceived as not being "safe", they are not naturally allowed. For most, the experience of being free of limiting, fear- based events does not exist. Often, some new input of happiness and joy is rejected because it comes under the broad limiting factor of "change". The "box" is the only comfortable place to be for the ego.

It is important to note that this is a naturally occurring aspect of the human condition and there is no blame concerning these normal reactions.

Dysfunctional early programming can at times lead to dangerous and even deadly results. This can occur by automatically reacting to dangerous circumstances poorly as well as creating a vibration of fear that will attract to ourselves the very thing we fear. As a minimum, this inflexibility limits freedom to change.

There is a concept shared in Glenda Green's book *Love Without End* that I would like to paraphrase here:

> The ego/mind works best within established and limited parameters. It must have two points of fixed reference in order to be operable. These two points are the past (experience) and the future. It projects past experience into the future to decide what actions to take in the present.

> The ego cannot deal with the concept of infinity. The heart (spirit) is centered around a viewpoint of infinity, and from this it draws its power to truly deal with life.

Another aspect of the ego, which is well known, is that of self-inflation, wherein a person will go on endlessly about how wonderful they are. This is obviously a cover-up reaction to a deep-seated feeling of inferiority. "You don't have to prove what you know is true" is the mechanism.

Again, the Circle of Experience tool will allow you to let go of beliefs that cause ego-inflation. An example would be any over self-inflating behavior. Such as:

A person keeps telling you how wonderfully they play an instrument when in fact you have heard them and it really isn't so good. What are they trying to prove that isn't true? That they are just wonderful. They also know this isn't true at some level. That there are many who are MUCH better. Their real belief, that is being over-compensated for, is that they believe that they are not good at all.

How can this be released? First by addressing your "truth" - that you are not good at all. Is this really true? The answer is – "No, I am not terminally terrible. I am learning and I like who I am, and SO WHAT that I am not "fabulous"? I love playing and am getting better with the practice. Who cares what someone else thinks, I LOVE me as I am now and that includes somewhat marginal playing skills. The key? Loving yourself <u>as you are</u> in the present, knowing you <u>are</u> doing the best you can with what you have, and finding your own joy in your playing.

One of the reasons the ego manifests this characteristic is because belonging to the group is perceived, at the genetic level, as being safe. The "safety" of actions that indicate this characteristic are that being "special" will get you accepted into the group. Not being "accepted" into the group will get you cast out, wherein you will die (this is the simplistic early-programming logic of the human). This kind of "logic" remains in place for life unless specifically addressed and changed.

Another specific action the ego takes that is worthy of note is the need to be RIGHT. This is a defense mechanism wherein if it is challenged or deemed wrong, it perceives it as an attack on its existence. We tend to identify with our ideas, philosophies and positions, so that being wrong about whatever the issue is, is tantamount to being attacked and ultimately losing one's deeply imbedded sense of independence and self.

The concept of taking a stand "to the death" comes from many places within the human psyche. Proving individuality is necessary to become a "productive" member of your group. Expressing territoriality (be it physical, emotional, intellectual or spiritual) is a genetically-driven natural protective action of humans. Powerful territoriality responses can manifest over such subjects as land, family, country, words, ideas, philosophical constructs, and positions on any subject.

The question arises as to what are the reasons we take these fixed (irrational?) positions. The simple answer is to keep us safely within the comfort zone of the box. This can be expanded to include fears of being unprepared or incapable of dealing with change. The box is "safe".

Trying to eliminate any of these fear responses is in itself a threat to the ego's sense of existence and safety and is tantamount to potential death. As you work harder to overcome the limitations, the ego perceives it as a specific threat to its existence because its safety (and theoretically yours) is in great danger. As you push harder the greater is the resistance and this can lead to dangerous conditions emanating from the life-threatening perception of the ego. "Like Vibrations Attract" can and does create some pretty hairy situations.

The intent is not to push too hard, but instead use a non-emotional approach that manifests in your non-angry responses to specific triggering events. Be gentle with yourself. ALL of you is doing the best you can with what you have. You would ask no more of anyone else.

<blockquote>ACT in your work with yourself,
Rather than RE-ACT.</blockquote>

In this natural process of becoming, it is the <u>feeling</u> of being safe that we seek, not actually being safe.

There is no mechanism within the ego to differentiate between that which was or is safe and that which is not. Fear becomes associated with being safe to such a degree that we begin to associate fear with being safe and therefore seek it out to create our "safe" reality. As mentioned above, a child of an alcoholic/abusive/hurtful environment will seek the safety of a similar "safe" (fear based) relationship. They will seek out a similar environment because it is perceived as love and safe. This behavioral response is a learned response that can be changed and "unlearned". In this case, fear becomes confused with, and identified as, love.

In line with this thinking, those who pursue conspiracies in every subject basically come from trusting no one, including themselves. This usually is a result of experiences in family or environment that have been harmful and require great diligence. It is a dark pursuit based on experience. Does this mean there are no conspiracies? Of course not, the question is what is the driving force behind the pursuit?

The ego is highly invested in maintaining the status quo, even if it is disquieting and painful to the rest of you. This is because it has established that it is relatively safe with things as they are. The ego has created a comfort zone and change would introduce new dangers which, it perceives, are worse than keeping the old patterns. The ego feels that it cannot deal with any change and will fail. Again, being aware of this

Change Your Reality

dichotomy can help you to bring perspective to the situation and potentially change in directions you would like. Well, you CAN deal with the problems of life! Look at yourself. You have! You are still here!

In finding difficulty in changing, you might run up against the situation where "no one tells me what to do, not even my own consciousness". One can become fully invested in a cause or position and will not change even when threatened with death. It is a matter of programming from levels that supersede the basic survival instincts of the individual. These are some of the reasons we take this position, they are all "survival of the species" issues:

It is territorial.
Playing the dominant male role in the "herd".
The "principle" of "it" is worth dying for.
Fight for the country.

Martyring oneself to a cause can serve a number of purposes for the human psyche. It can serve the ego's need to be productive and therefore to be safe within the tribe. It can be the result of seeing that loyalty to a cause will help us to belong as well. It can create a feeling of importance. For all of these and many more, it is ego-created on the basis of perceived safety.

These established safety patterns often include major behavioral patterns such as listed below from James Redfield's *The Celestine Prophecy*. By being aware whether some of these are the way you act, you might decide that such behaviors no longer serve the way you choose to manifest. The patterns here are described from my perspective.

"Aloof": A person coming from a place of aloof is coming from a state of fear that they have everything to hide because they know the "truth" and the "truth" is that they have no value. They maintain their distance so that no one can get close.

"Interrogator": A person using this pattern, is establishing their position to "prove what they know isn't true". That they are better than you (which is a cover-up of their "real" truth). They will question everything to keep focus away from themselves.

"Intimidator": From this position, a person is again in the "proving" mode and saying that if I can intimidate you and make you feel inferior, then I will "prove" that I am superior. It is a very common practice to see someone put someone else down. The real purpose of this action is to make one's <u>self</u> feel important or better, obviously something the person does not really believe.

"Poor me": Perhaps the most honest of the traits, for in fact this person does feel they are intimidated by everything and the "victim" of circumstances. However, the real issue here is a feeling of total powerlessness in the face of reality.

> You are not a VICTIM of your reality,
> you CREATE it.

Each of these traits comes from a lack of self-worth. They are all behavior patterns that we can do something about. Recognizing them, we can use them as "ins" to changing our image of ourselves.

Some of the patterns that last for lifetimes are in regard to our health. Being "sick" as a child bought us attention, love and the safety of knowing we belonged. It got us out of school and served many purposes of getting us what we wanted. This pattern can become so ingrained that, while on the surface you want to be well, the ego can't change without significant intervention by you in the present.

Throwing tantrums also proved useful to get what we wanted and this trait may well still be in use.

Change Your Reality

In deciding to change some of these patterns, you have to be aware that they are about to "bubble up" and consciously take control. Stop the re-action and replace it with a desired action.

If you cannot stop the reaction, the realization that you just got "triggered" offers an opportunity for you to respond to yourself. First by not coming down on yourself, and then saying – non-emotionally - "Next time I shall do better." This sets up a very real intent to change, with the knowledge that you are a work-in-progress, and doing just fine!

Although these expressions of the ego are an integral part of the whole, the ego also can perceive itself as a separate part whose job is to keep us safe - including from our self. Herein resides a potential problem. The conscious desires may significantly differ from the programmed "acceptable and safe" behaviors of the past.

In identifying itself as separate, the ego takes on an autonomy of its own. It is now concerned with its own safety and in time this becomes more important than the host's. Now, to validate its existence, it must defend itself to the death. This can easily result from an antagonistic relation with yourself as you grew up. Awareness and commitment to change can help in creating the "new" you.

As a result of all this, having chosen to change, we are faced with the problem of modifying the ego's response to become in sync with our conscious mind and desires.

Remember: From our position of working with the ego, we are NOT in battle. The ego is just doing what it is set up to do. You, as the programmer, have the job of the reprogramming. Do you get angry with your computer when it needs "help"? Well, maybe so, but you get the idea.

How do you do this? There are many paths, each one personal to the person searching. The tools to achieve this end are shared in previous chapters; however, a general approach can be outlined which might be of value:

1. Desire.
   You have to want to change.
2. Intent.
   Harmony of self with self.
   WE are together in this.
   Peace in the process and with the unfolding.
3. Attitude.
   The quest is not hopeless.
   We can do this.
   One step at a time.
   Patience - this will take time.
   Be at peace with the process.

Know that the ego needs both to feel comfortable being an individual and safe in its belonging to the whole of you.

You need to feel totally comfortable being independent in your life.

4. Knowledge.
   Knowledge is power.
   Understanding how it all works.
5. Action.
   Be conscious in the present.
   Pursue diligently.

Be patient and consistent. Know that this is a reprogramming of the driving mechanism that have been "how you operate" for your whole life.

Use the feeling exercises (Chapter 4) to bring the feeling of unconditional love towards the ego and the child. Feel the safety and warmth of that love and tell the child (out loud) that you love it and will keep it safe.

Reiterate to the child that you, as an adult, are now the parent of yourself and are best equipped to know what will keep you both safe. The feeling of this truth is paramount because the ego cannot respond to thought; it responds to feelings. The thought part of the brain was not functioning when the ego was formed.

Use the term "we".

6. Take control.

Remind the ego that you, the adult, are in charge. That you are not a child, that you have much greater capabilities to "run the show" now than "we" did as a child. "We" will make life decisions from the point of consciousness in the present. "We have grown up, and learned and changed, yet we are still one person - always have been and always will be".

7. Perseverance.
Never give up!!!

Generally speaking, the ego makes a lousy master and a great workmate and partner. The object of interrelating with the ego is to integrate its operational paradigms with those of our selves as adults. This is possible and it isn't a battle. Make an "enemy" of the ego and try to destroy it and all that will be accomplished is indeed battle - and you, the adult, will lose, for survival to the ego is paramount. The ego is a non-conscious function of our being and has 500,000 times the "computing" capability of your conscious mind. (Remember Bruce Lipton's *The Biology of Belief* 40 to 20,000,000 ratio?). So it is not only a really good idea to bring that power into harmony with your conscious desires, it is a necessity.

In all this work, you will find yourself talking to your self, bringing "reason", intent and desire to the work of change. In standard psychological terms, this is called Cognitive Behavioral Therapy (CBT). In this work, it is paramount to understand that the ego is a <u>feeling</u> aspect of your personality. The "truth" of any "logical left brain reasoning" must be <u>felt</u>.

The ego has to hold the set of belief systems it has in place because collectively they (beliefs and behavior patterns) have "proved" to keep us safe. There is no differentiation between one belief and all of them because from a child's point of view it is "all or nothing". Any assault upon "sacred" beliefs will be met with stonewalling.

Poor self-worth is generally at the core of that part of the ego that we are working to change. Feeling "powerless" is based on the very real fact that as a baby and very young child you ARE powerless. Information from the earliest experiences shows us that we are powerless, helpless, useless and have no real value. Pretty heavy, but true.

Traditionally this absoluteness is ameliorated over time, but in so many cases, lack of self worth lasts a lifetime and manifests in all kinds of behaviors that are difficult to address. As life progresses we are told by others through actions or words and, by ourselves, through judgment, that we are of little or no value and consequently we come to totally believe it at a very deep level. These deep-seated sets of beliefs is the playground of the non-consciousness and must be defended to the death - sometimes literally. What to do?

The idea is to reprogram the non-consciousness. If the ego can feel safe, then it will cease to make up problems to make itself "feel" safe. This is true for all the name-calling you direct towards yourself. Another point to pursue is to have the childhood ego feel safe with the adult having the power to make decisions as indicated in number 6 above. In other words, we are talking about integration of intentions and goals between the non-conscious part of us and the conscious part of us. This includes the elimination of many behavior patterns that are currently non-productive or destructive.

If you'll notice, we are basically saying that personality and ego are really inseparable. Successfully deal with one and the other will follow. Then the question arises whether the ego and personality are different. The answer is that the ego manifests as behavior patterns and the personality is behavior patterns that are time and situation dependent, so for the purposes of release of limiting programming, they are inseparable. Deal with one, you are dealing with both.

Easily the most difficult obstacle on the path of reprogramming is self worth. We naturally grow up judging ourselves in everything we do and very often find ourselves "wanting". The world around us tends to add fuel to this "judgment" by telling us how "less" we are than everyone else. While we may have support for a good self-image, usually the ideas that "stick" are the ones that support our beliefs in our own deficiencies.

We perceive ourselves as 'imperfect". This is a falsehood. That judgment is based on the human, and your own, concept of what "perfection " is. The truth is that you are Perfect" as you are now as viewed from the "Cosmic" viewpoint. Review again the concept of perfection as defined in Chapter 1.

There are two main reasons for this situation that come from the nature of the human condition. The first is the natural need to judge something as safe. We do this from the very first breath as a baby. It is built in as a survival instinct and resides in the reptilian brain from the history of our species. The second is more devious but much more important and it is the magical thinking of childhood that makes goals we set for ourselves impossible to achieve. Even being a superhero is not BIG enough.

The latter sets up behavior patterns that last a lifetime and may cover many aspect of our lives, such as not rich enough, not pretty enough, not strong enough, not young enough, not something enough, or not anything enough.

When burdened with this magical thinking, you can never be "good enough" to be free. There is always the need to have done more, earned more, spent 10 years in Tibet, taken enough courses in some subject and so on. The list will never end on what you MUST additionally do to make it OK to be OK.

Remember this is YOUR idea and judgment of what is necessary to be free of limiting programming, not anyone else's and certainly not that of the Universe.

Now, with all that, what DO we do? We apply the tools given in Chapter 4. Start with the "Circle of Experience". What is it you believe at the ego level?

That you:
    Haven't done enough?
    Haven't earned the position desired?
    Aren't good enough?

Are:
    Unsafe ?
    Useless ?
    Powerless ?
    Hopeless ?
    Have no value ?
    Are a failure ?
    Bad?
    and on and on.

Be sure to add your own "known" "truths".

In every case you deal with the belief from the two attitudes:

1. Is that necessarily true?
   And
2. SO WHAT?
   Say to your self:

"That trait, whatever it is, is an integral part of how I manifest. I LOVE me as I am NOW." Know that you are doing the best you can under the specific circumstances that prevail at any time. This is true for the past, present and the future.

Keep in mind that these "beliefs" you now consider negative are an integral part of your psyche and sometimes it is actually useful to use them. The difference resulting from this work is that you can call on them by choice instead of "knee jerk" into them automatically.

If you think about it, all the "names" you have called yourself actually can be of value depending on circumstances, so "eliminating" a trait is not necessarily a good idea. All of these traits can be held in storage for use if you consciously choose to bring them forth. What does this say? "All the names I called myself are an integral part of what I am and I LOVE that, so I'll keep them as potential capabilities."

Example?
"not something enough". Continuing to learn is always a good idea.
"stupid". Sometimes playing "stupid" gets good results.
"vain". Nothing "wrong" with looking nice.
"manipulative". Well, there are times- it is all choice.

Could you have done better?
Should you have done differently?
Would you have done so if you could?

Well, children of the Universe, the universal answer is "no". You might have liked it to be different, but it wasn't. Time to let go of the judgment, forgive yourself for being you, and move on to love yourself as you are.

If a belief or pattern comes from a traumatic experience, use the "De-energizing Technique" for potential release.

Once again, you have the kinesiological and pendulum approaches to determine "yes" and "no" answers in your quest.

As an example, when I use it to determine my "real" feelings on a matter, I use it in this manner:

Let's say I have just come from an encounter with a person named Steve. There was an emotional response telling me there is something to be addressed. It wasn't very pleasant, and I'm not sure what was going on. I want to find out, so I decide to use the pendulum. I find a place where I can be alone and proceed.

First a statement of the situation: i.e. "I am unhappy about the encounter with Steve." (This focuses on a particular point for the work.)

A. The pendulum should be swinging in a "yes" direction.

Q: Do I know what it is that's bothering me?

A: The answer will probably be "yes".

I have some initial thoughts as to what the irritation might be, so I start with them.

Q: Is it his attitude?
A: No.
Q: Is it that he is pushy?
A: No.

You might have been sure that it was pushy but it isn't, so try to think of other things about him that bothered you.

Q: Is it that he was arrogant?
A: No.

So you're stumped. Say to yourself: "This is me I'm talking to. I can bring to my mind what it is, so let's do that." Think and let some ideas come to mind and then ask.

Never let yourself be angry or you will only go into other patterns and not get where you want to go. You are not being stupid or slow in this process. Look at those judgments for their source and eliminate them later. So proceed.

Q: Is it that he was distant?

A: Yes.

Q: What does his being "distant" make me feel like? Insignificant?

Note here that I am thinking "out loud" to myself, but eventually come to a single point - the word "insignificant". This is important because now we are going to label the feeling.

A: No.

Hmmm. (thinking - "give me a clue".)

Q: Unimportant?

Note: To a child the difference between "insignificant" and "unimportant" may well be real. Definitions may be very subtle, or not. They are how YOU interpret them, not someone else.

A: Yes.

OK. How old am I that I feel this way? Bring an age to mind. Is it 5?

A: No.

Q: Around there?

A: Yes.

Q: 6?

A: Yes.

Q: Did something happen in first grade that made me feel "unimportant"?

A: Yes.

OK. Bring it to mind.

It is highly likely that you will remember an incident that occurred then. If you don't, then let yourself "imagine" an incident and see what happens. Begin to ask questions. Let's assume no particular image comes to mind.

Q: Was it at home?
A: No.
Q: Was it at school?
A: Yes.
Q: Did it happen in class?
A: Yes.

Here you can probably come up with a scenario that might be emotionally powerful for a 6 year old.

Q: Was it where I was prepared and in front of class and someone "upstaged" me and I was forgotten?
A: Yes.

This CAN be an emotionally traumatic incident for a 6 year old and can raise feelings of inadequacy and lead to feeling unimportant and outcast - even for a lifetime. Now for the release. It is important here to "feel" the emotions of that age and totally empathize with yourself as that child. Still using the pendulum:

Q: So it lead me to believe that I am unimportant?
A: (probably) Yes.

Taka a hint and go a little further.

Q: Did it also make me feel useless?
A: (potentially) No.
Q: Unlovable?
A: No.
Q: Of no value?
A: Yes.
Q: Are either of those absolutely true?
Unimportant?
A: No.
Of no value?

A: No.

The "Circle of Experience" needs to be broken, so in each of the "realizations" above, you need to ask yourself if in fact, you have never been "unimportant", and if you have never been "of no value". In both cases you certainly have had corresponding experiences in which you WERE important and WERE useful.

Proceeding:

Q: Can I understand at this age, that it was just an experience and that what happened wasn't directed at me and even if it were, that if it happened now, it wouldn't bother me?

A: (hopefully) Yes.

Q: Can I let this go and realize that I am not "unimportant"?

A: Yes. (The thought comes to mind I still think Steve is a stinker.)

Q: That's OK, Steve was just being Steve. Do we still believe we are "unimportant"?

A: No.

Q: Of no value?

A: No.

If either answer was "Yes", then it opens a door that begins with the question: What is the source of my feeling?

Now, the question arises as to whether you accomplished anything. The measure is that if you have a similar stimulus in the future, you have this same emotional reaction to "unimportant", or "of no value". If not, then you have "got it". If you do, then go back into one of the internal communication systems again. You will achieve your goal through persistence.

The above example is simple, yet very real and important. There are many paths that a process like the above could take and there is not room here to go into the possibilities. That is why you have to take charge of the search and resultant process.

The goal of any one session is to arrive at - "I no longer believe that something is 'wrong' with me, or I want to change that", because the limiting programming has been eliminated.

The second part of the release was shared before and that is: "That personality trait is an inherent part of how I manifest and what went to make me "me". AND I like me as I am, so - SO WHAT? I shall keep the capability of that particular trait in reserve in case there is a time it is appropriate to use - and I, at a conscious level, shall determine when and if that might be."

Fear is the paradigm from which we often come. We are naturally there. It is our goal to move beyond this limitation to a greater understanding of self in a spirit of joy and love, without harm to any aspect of our being.

Remember again that the wonderful experiences we have had have also generated behavior patterns we are not addressing in this work. Know that you are joy as well. Hopefully learning is a rewarding and joyful experience for you.

Here I would like to present an idea that may occur to you in the natural process of looking at the initiating events in your past. Events that caused you stress and resulting limiting programming are brought forward, sometimes in sequence, to be released. As a result of these adventures into consciousness, you may find that you feel ashamed of your behavior, and it just won't go away. Intellectually you may know the perspective that needs to be brought to the situation, but you still feel ashamed. What do you do?

It is a good idea to ask forgiveness for what you "did" to others and at this juncture, for yourself as well. In simple terms, you are sorry this ever happened and would just as soon have had someone else provide the learnings, however, it did happen, and you know there was "purpose". Feel the "sorry" and proceed as follows:

Using the pendulum or kinesiological approach, work on the feeling of being ashamed. First set your intent, which is to release the feeling of being ashamed, or at least bringing it down to a reasonable level. Second, use the Circle of Experience to let the resulting beliefs (I am a bad person, etc.) be brought into perspective. ("No, you are not always "bad"). Next use the De-energizing technique (Chapter 4) to reduce the "ashamed" feeling. It might go like this:

On a scale of one to ten, how bad is the "ashamed" feeling? (let's say it is a ten).

Now bring some perspective to the situation, such as:

This was an important part of my growth.

It helped make me into the person I am today. (good, right?)

The other person/ situation provided a learning potential for all.

I had no control over the situation due to my automatic programming.

Like vibrations attracted each of us to this situation for purpose.

There was a "gift" here. What was it?

On a scale of one to seven, How much do you believe these points?

(hopefully a seven)

Now go back to the "ashamed" feeling. How "ashamed" do you feel?

It should have reduced significantly in number. Perhaps a two or three? If not, add additional perspective ideas until the number is low enough for you. Continue this process until the "ashamed feeling" is reduced to an acceptable level for you. You test this by bringing the event to mind again and seeing if you still "feel" ashamed.

This can obviously be used for any "negative" response to a situation that you want to "let go".

There is a natural resistance to change that can manifest in a number of internal patterns. It comes from feeling that the known is safer than the unknown, and from the reptilian-brain level, this is true. The resistance can vary from mild to severe, depending on the initial emotional situation.

Lying, by the non-conscious part of us, is not being "difficult". It is always a defense mechanism. We are running from fears - so many and so pervasive. Often a search will go through many layers and much time to get to what is "really going on". Dreams are an example of the way we disguise the truth.

The use of the pendulum or the kinesiological approach can help you to find out what is going on in small matters as well. The human animal has the tendency to displace actual fears on something external so as to relieve some of the tension that a situation creates. We also use dreams for this purpose.

Being anxious about a situation that doesn't warrant any anxiety (such as going to the store) is often a trigger for displacing concern over something entirely different. I might be waiting for a delivery and I get butterflies in my stomach. This seems entirely unwarranted, and I wonder if this is what the anxt is really about. So I go to the pendulum and ask. It is almost always something different. Usually it is anxiety over the process and actually allowing myself to move forward. What triggers the questioning is the illogicality of being so anxious over something that is essentially inconsequential.

At this point, I would like to share one of the most difficult patterns I had to deal with in my own process, for the story might be of some value to you in yours. I mentioned before that I had rheumatic fever when I was a child and that this illness was pivotal. One of the most pervasive and long-lasting patterns, for which I could not find the cause, was my continuing to make up answers to my own questions. Another was the seeming continuing duality of me and me, a separation of needed and needy, always dependent on someone else. Singing song phrases such as "I won't last a day without you" was one of the subliminal indications that this separation continued to exist. Early one morning I was thinking about a subject and asked for an answer. The answer I got was obviously not true and was made up. The fact that it was "obviously made up" indicated, among other things, that part of me wanted to be "found out". I immediately went into the feeling and, using the pendulum, stated that it was made up, wasn't it? The answer was "yes". I then asked:

Q: How old am I that I made up the answer?
A: 5.

Having been here many times before, I knew pretty well where to go from here.

Q: Was it in school?
A: Yes.

At this point I went into trying to empathize with my emotional condition in kindergarten at age 5, and had the strong feeling of needing to be recognized. So I asked:

Q: Is it that I "had" to be recognized?
A: Yes.

Q: Was I desperate? (I could feel this desperation)
A: Yes.

I had to try to think "what could make me so desperate at 5 years of age?" There were other kids in the class, why was it so important that I continuously get the attention? I wasn't stupid. I have found over time, that questions bring answers; one only has to have a question to get an answer.

The answer came to me that I needed it to survive. But what could make this so powerful a need? What is the link? The whole picture fell into place. Because of the disease. I was terrified of it ever happening again. It was obviously a life-threatening disease. Mother made it plain that she was frightened, so I was too. It was also obvious that mother needed to be present all the time to protect me from it happening again and keep me "quiet". When I lost this total care from mother, I sought it outside. The intensity of needing 100 percent attention was not available in school or anywhere else and I felt severely threatened. It was indeed a survival response and

I was terrified. I continued the pattern of requiring inordinate attention for most of my life but ameliorated it by developing another internal pattern.

This pattern was one of separation of self into the protector and the protected. It was a problem I had been addressing for years but never got to the source. There were many factors which created an apparent duality of nature, some of which have been mentioned before but this was the first time-wise, and most powerful. It was truly at the source.

So I pursued the need to have total care as follows:

Q: Do I believe that I must have someone around (mother) to keep me safe?

A: Yes.

Q: Is this absolutely true?

A: No.

Q: Can I FEEL the "truth" of this statement? Are there times when I do NOT need someone else around to feel safe? (such as watching TV, eating, etc.)

A: Yes.

Q: Are there in fact times when I feel safer if I am alone?

A: Yes.

What comes to mind while working on this is that it was true at one time but that is no longer the case. The fact is that I am no longer a child and often prefer to be alone and feel perfectly safe.

Q: So do I still believe that I need someone to watch over me, tell me what to do and keep me safe?

A: No.

It is the removal of the driving core belief that releases the pattern. This will always be the case. If the pattern comes up again, then there is something else which feeds the pattern as well. A question to ask after this kind of release is:

Q: Is there any other reason why I must still need someone to take care of me and tell me what to do?

A: No.

If the answer were "yes", it could be many things and lead to additional corridors of knowledge about yourself. Certainly your path will be different than mine.

Basically what I am presenting in this book is the distillation of many years of processing in a most obsessive manner. This was a pattern in itself and I was driven by needing to know how everything works to make myself feel safe.

The constructs of a child's mind to keep safe are unlimited in their creativity. Facades of all types and behavior patterns of separate personalities are but a few of the possibilities. It is called "magical thinking", and has much more breadth than you, as an adult, would bring to a situation.

There is a mechanism that some children do after having had a particularly difficult experience. It is "quitting". "Quitting" occurs when there has been a situation that occurs that was so "terrible" for you that you "quit" and turned your life over to another you. That "you", the "new" you then proceeded to live your life.

Know that first of all it is a defense mechanism for survival. In the psyche, you, the person "quitting", gives up all responsibility for continuing to deal with life. The "new" you is given responsibility for carrying on the job of living. This "new" person will have some alteration of personality that, in the eyes of the "quitter", makes them different enough to cope with life. The "quitter" is left behind at whatever age the event occurred that caused the quitting reaction.

This "new" you may be very similar (as seen by others) to the "old" you, but to the "quitter", the difference is sufficient to allow for continuing life, rather than doing something more drastic. In some cases, the "new" you is significantly different and can be looked at by others as an alternative personality.

In fact, of course, it is still you. At some time in the future (perhaps this present) you may have to go back and reintegrate these parts because they will resist changing due to feeling "left behind".

How do you do this?

First there is the intent to "reintegrate" your self. Next you go back to the causal event in your mind and "feel" the intensity of being overwhelmed by circumstances. The "part" of you that is feeling left behind will be at the age of the event. Then you tell your self (at that age) that no part of you will be left behind. Feel the truth of this and bring forth a corresponding compassion for your self. Do this as the adult. Tell that "part" of your self that it was never left behind, because it is with you now, and has come up into consciousness many times, and in this way has always been present with you. Then feel the truth that there is no longer needs to be any separation. Again, tell your self that you love this "part" of you and "they" are a necessary and integral aspect of the total you and are no longer separate. Dwell on the feelings for a little while. Let it out. This part of you has been in a prison of its own making for years. You may find yourself crying. This is good.

Once this escape mechanism has been created, you may find several times you used it to feel safe. Under some circumstances, multiple personalities can result and these need to be addressed one at a time. In like manner, even small incidents that seemingly resulted in no personality changes must be separately addressed. This "rescue mission" can actually be fun, as well as rewarding.

It should be noted here that this is not everyone's path. It is a special situation that is brought to you for informational purposes. Your creational path is only yours and it is expected that only some of the potential situations mentioned in this book apply to you.

There is nothing "wrong" with an emotional response and being a child is part of what we are. Why would we want to lose the ability to wonder at beauty or some new gadget? Why should we want to give up having giggle fits? Why should we want to not do anything that was fun as a kid, if we can do it now? The idea here is not to deny your childhood, only to remove limiting patterns, put it all in perspective and find the joy in it again. Personally, I love silly. Think on this:

> You are never too old
> to have a happy childhood.

I carry the pendulum around with me all the time because something might come up I would like to address and release, but mostly because I am totally fascinated with how we work. Stimuli for "Where did THAT come from?" are actually fun to pursue. When I don't have the pendulum with me, I use the "Applied Kinesiology" approach, since I always have my fingers available.

I would like to share another example with you because the situation is so pervasive amongst us all.

A number of years ago, I was visiting my mother at her house and was unloading the dishwasher. She came over to help me and I snapped that I could do it. She was taken aback and stepped back and let me finish. Later I asked myself "Where did THAT come from?" Pendulum time.

Statement: I just snapped at my mother in a very mean way almost pushing her away.
A: Yes.
Q: Do I know what that is about?
A: Yes.
Q: Is it about her pestering me?
A: No.
Q: Is it about being right or wrong in what I was doing?
A: No.

Hmmm. Going back into the situation and recalling the emotionals, I felt I needed to prove something. Well that seemed easy then.

Q: Did I need to prove I was independent of her now and could do things myself?
A: Yes.
Q: So, I believe I needed her approval to do things and yet was also still dependent?
A: Yes.
Q: Well I've grown up considerably, do I still need her approval?
A: Yes.

The thoughts come to mind relatively quickly as I pursue this course of questioning.

Q: It is because of the illness and her keeping me safe?
A: Yes.
Q: Am I ill any more, and do I still need her protection?
A: (Just a little movement in the no direction.)
Q: I am very reluctant to give this up?
A: Yes.

Statement: At this point, mother can no longer take care of me. I have been off by myself for many years and have taken on the job of keeping myself safe. I am a continuous stream of consciousness and it is me, in the present, that can do the best job of keeping me safe.

Q: Based on experience, can I take better care of me than mother can?
A: Yes.
Q: Do I need to let this soak into my hologram, for it is actually quite significant?
A: Yes.

The following morning I asked again:

Q: Do I believe I need mother's protection to keep me safe?
A: No.

It worked, and subsequent patterns confirmed that indeed it did work.

Change Your Reality

The following has been mentioned before, however, it is worth repeating.

Your ego is designed to use the neurological nature of your physical being. It does this very well. It responds from the reasoning basis of experience. The ego takes time to respond to a stimulus such as a question. Your intuition needs no such time and knows the answers to questions you may ask. The intuitional response is the "first impulse". It comes from the heart - your true intelligence. Make it a habit to listen for this "first impulse" and learn to trust it. Only personal experiences will show you how often it is the best answer. Practice trusting your intuition.

It appears that as we have grown up, the ego may take on an agenda of its own. Survival of itself is more important than even survival of you as an individual. It seems totally counterproductive, but from the view of the way the ego became what it is, it makes perfect sense.

In working to grow out of the early childhood patterns, it can help to see whether you and your ego find it incomprehensible to think that you could grow into the "incredible" person you are today. Feel whether this might be true for you. If it is, tell your little self that it IS true. All the terrible things you judged yourself as being may even have been true at the time, but you did grow and change and add new information and perspectives. Just look at your body and see the changes. Your emotional, mental and spiritual parts have changed as well. Welcome your little self to the present with open and loving arms.

Another point to think about is the relationship between the ego and the child. Often the differentiation will not be obvious. This is because the ego receives much of its programming inputs when we are children. An effective approach to dealing with these child-created protective patterns is to give the child a job. That job is to be a child and bring forth the fun and silliness and joy and wonder of a child's experiences, and leave the decision-making to the adult you have become. Tell yourself that it is you, as an adult in the present, that has the greatest amount of information and therefore the greatest capability of keeping you safe. Tell your child-self that you REALLY need and value the capability to feel joy because you want lots more fun in your life.

An additional mechanism that is worth addressing is in regards to imagination. You might find yourself imagining and "scripting" disastrous outcomes to your desired future. This is usually done subliminally and manifests lots of reasons not to do something. This is used as a defense mechanism for the ego and the feeling is that if you give up imagining these outcomes, you will not be safe in this scripted future. In other words, doing nothing is the only "safe" path. Thus significant resistance is offered by this mechanism to achieving your dreams. Disaster scenarios are destructive on at least two levels. First, "like vibrations attract" will potentially create the disaster. Second, the mechanism keeps you from achieving the freedom and joy you desire.

To eliminate this mechanism it is necessary to convince yourself that these scenarios, and the fear of change, have not kept you safe in the past and actually have created unhappiness and even "disasters". You need to find and <u>feel</u> the "truth" of this for yourself to emotionally release the "need" to be safe by creating these destructive scenarios.

There are some deep-seated, limiting programming beliefs worth addressing that are common significant hurdles to overcome.

The first is the feeling of being powerless. It stems from the truth of our powerless condition when we are babies and stays with us at a deep level for a lifetime. As long as we measure our power from the point of view of "how much", we are always going to find ourselves lacking, which reinforces our belief that we are not powerful "enough". If we accept Like Vibrations

Change Your Reality

Attract as the true way our universe operates, then we are 100% powerful in creating our reality and its not only true for you, but every human being on the planet. Can't get any better or more powerful than that. In fact, this approach is the only way you can know that you are indeed powerful.

This is indeed one of the most powerful arguments you can bring to yourself as a child that seems to be working to prove how powerful it is. While it is really coming from the "truth" that it is (you don't have to prove what you know is true) powerless. The TRUTH is that that part of you, all along the way, has been THE creative energy of your existence and indeed totally powerful. Take that kiddo!

Another belief that permeates our existence is that asking "God" for something personal is not allowed. This kind of "selfish" behavior gets one punished, so the ego perceives that this is a very bad idea. In fact, if one believes that the universal machine is impersonal and needs instructions, then who or what is going to punish you? The answer is YOU, because of your belief that you should be punished. In the simplest terms, every thought you have is an instruction, a "prayer" to the Universe, to "God".

Do you expect to be punished by your car when you start it and set off for some desired location? The car does what it is "instructed" to do by you and there is no question concerning your having chosen a destination. In like manner, the Universe is your vehicle to wherever you want to go and has no "agenda" of its own. This attitude decisively eliminates any measure of "worth" needed to achieve your dreams, AND eliminates any possibility of punishing you for your choices. Life is all choice – yours! In fact, the Universe will not choose for you what "should" happen. It is entirely up to you. You naturally create your reality as a result of your vibration from some level of your psyche as explained in Chapter 2. The idea is to now make those choices consciously, and reprogram those patterns and beliefs that are not in concert with your current desires.

Bringing the ego and personality back into harmony with your conscious desires is totally possible and very rewarding. Your buddyrole awaits. Unconditional love of yourself WITH your ego is on the path to achieving your goal of being free of limiting programming. After all, your child, your ego, didn't have the capabilities of rewiring that you do. It takes desire, consistency, work, awareness and focus on your goals to make it happen. Begin with loving and trusting yourself.

Don't ever give up!

Chapter 6

DREAMS

A very important tool in identifying your source of fears and causal events is your dreams. Many psychologists consider them the golden door to our psyche. They are that and more. Your dreams have a multifunctional purpose in your life. Dreams release inner tensions, rewire your hologram and give you wonderful insights into what is internally going on. They can also be "messages" that inform you of future possibilities.

The interpretation of dreams is often the problem when it isn't entirely clear what the pink elephant and other strange events may have symbolized. Here are some points that may help you.

1. Dreams are generally of two types: self-generated and informational.
2. The self-generated dreams are a result of your internal workings. You DO know what they mean; you only have to think on it.
3. The language of your non-conscious is symbols. These symbols are made up by you, so you do know what they represent. You just have to work with them.
4. There are no universal dream symbols.

5. There are, however, archetypical beings such as the teacher, old wise man, warrior and many others. These are part of the Jungian collective-unconscious concept.
6. Dream symbolism is a function of what you have experienced. If you have read books on dream symbolism, you will incorporate that symbolism in your dream work because you have come to believe that they are true. If not, then you will make up your own, based on your experience.
7. You are often all the characters in the dream. This certainly is true for the main characters. The dream may express your multifaceted feelings towards any given situation and is a good clue as to your true attitude.

Note: That you are the major players in the dream is a very important concept in interpreting dreams. You, as you and you, will play both sides of the issue, each bringing important perspectives and understanding to the situations depicted. This approach should be one of the first thoughts brought to the dream interpretation process. Which one of the main characters are you consciously in the dream. This is important.

8. Your non-conscious very often calls upon stimuli from the specific events and circumstances which occurred during that day and then adds the story line to give you the dream. Recognizing this can explain some of the seemingly strange contexts.

All dreams are "informational", that is, giving us information with which to work, however, in a broader sense there are dreams which have "messages" that are direct information and do not need interpretation. Their meaning is usually straightforward. This is what is referred to as number 2 above.

We are primarily focusing in this work on information that needs interpretational effort to be of value.

Both Jung and Freud wrote extensively about dream work. While their bodies of work overlap, there are significant differences as well. In my case, Robert Johnson's book *Inner Work*, which is based on Jungian concepts, remains one of the more powerful learning mediums for dream work. Jung's concept of the collective unconscious closely parallels the idea that we are individuals in the sea of Oneness.

There is an additional Jungian concept that is shared in Robert Johnson's *Inner Work*, called "Active Imagination". While regular dream work is passive in the sense that you analyze but generally do not play a conscious part in its creation, in "Active Imagination" you are an active creator and draw information from your non-conscious – on purpose, and with purpose.

This is the way it works. Imagine yourself in a very comfortable place. It can be an actual place you have available or have visited, or an imaginary place. Actually sit down on a comfortable bench or chair for this work. Then imagine that in this place you have created there is a path that allows others to come by and visit.

First set your intent. Ask someone to come visit you from your non-conscious mind. You want some aspect of yourself to come forth, not an external entity. For instance - "would someone like to come forth to share something with me?" Be patient, especially in the first few times you work with the system.

Wait for a little while and someone will show up. Keep your questioning, analytical mind, quiet and accept the first impulse - the first image, and allow it to become relatively clear.

It will not be the same as having someone in the room with you, for it will be totally a function of your imagination. Solidity is not the goal, awareness is.

Ask them why they have come and what they have to share with you. The answers may come in your own voice or simply a thought, it doesn't matter. Have a conversation. You may be surprised as to what they will share. You may not agree with them and can say so, but what counts is that you have brought forth some beliefs in the form of an interactive image that have been in your non-conscious mind for some time. The individuals or groups can be archetypes (leader, warrior, father, teacher) or just individuals representing some aspect of your thoughts about yourself. They can also be another aspect of you from another life. No matter what goes on, it is an opportunity for you to hear something about yourself and interact. Remember this is a dream, an imagining, so anything goes. It is not some real person, it is a thought made interactive. Results can be interesting.

What if it doesn't work? You may be trying too hard. This is not a test and there are no performance criteria. Relax and try again some other time. You have introduced the concept into your mind.

Some are able to have "lucid" dreams. These are dreams in which you are actually consciously aware of what is going on and can change them as they proceed. These are particularly useful as you can "watch" yourself reacting to situations and later analyze what changes you made and why. Remembering what was in a "lucid" dream is usually relatively easy.

Some say they don't dream. This is unlikely. REM (Rapid Eye Movement) sleep indicates that dreams are in progress.

Remembering your dreams is often a problem, as they tend to fade quickly. A dream journal, either verbal (a voice-activated recorder) or written, can be helpful but is not always necessary. Often you can get the meaning upon awakening and make a determination as to whether it is of value to you or not.

If remembering dreams is very difficult for you, you might ask if there are some core beliefs about dreams that preclude your being aware of them. These can be: Dreams are bad, dangerous, scary, stupid, not worth anything or whatever might exist from your experiential background. If so, eliminate the belief by using the "Circle of Experience". Some deny they dream because as a child they had nightmares and dreams are very scary. Use the "Circle of Experience" release to allow yourself to acknowledge that indeed you do dream and can actually enjoy working with and learning from them.

Upon awakening, the first question to ask yourself is whether you are supposed to get something from this dream or is it just a natural part of the rearranging process. Many times it will be the former and sometimes the latter. If the dream interpretation is just too complex, don't dwell on it. Ask for another dream that will be clearer. It is often of value to take small portions of the dream to work on at a time. In this mode the rest of the dream meanings will often fall into place.

Nightmares are the most disturbing dreams by far. They are also the greatest potential learning mechanisms, for they bring up the deeply fear-based programming we have been dealing with for a lifetime. They will often be reoccurring dreams with issues that are begging to be dealt with and released. The "De-energizing Technique" may be of value in bringing the situations into perspective and lessening their emotional impact. As mentioned before in relation to this, if the trauma is too great to be able to handle, a trained professional is definitely recommended.

One helpful attitude towards lessening the trauma of the dream is to remind yourself that the content of the dream has come forth to be dealt with, and it is a gift. Also along this line, knowing that the nightmare is an integral part of your growth process can help you to keep it all in perspective. When, upon awakening, searching for the meaning of the nightmares becomes your desired path, the fear-based power of the content will most likely not be as intense. Then you can begin the interpretation and release.

The first step upon awakening from the nightmare or any dream is to be aware that you are OK. Then start thinking about what went on and how does it relate to your present-life situation. What is it telling you? To achieve an understanding of the interactional aspects and their relation to your present life you need to allow yourself to ask questions. Sometimes using the kinesiological approach or the pendulum to get "yes" and "no" answers will help considerably. For instance:

Was it about this? If not, was it this? The approach would be the same as questioning yourself about the source of the emotional reaction you had when an event occurred in your waking life. Just by asking questions you start yourself on the path of finding the answers as well as releasing the energies associated with the dream. The mind will use this first question to begin the quest, and then the release.

Explore every aspect of the dream, for every aspect does in fact have related meaning. As you get down below the major messages, simple things like the nature of the wallpaper or placement of furniture (etc.) may tell you something interesting and even fun.

The specific interpretations are so varied and personal that it would be impossible to make a dream list. The symbolism used is totally yours. There are many professionals who can help you with understanding your dreams, but I would suggest that you can become very adept at doing it yourself if you take the time and make the effort.

It is highly probable that you have had the experience of holding a problem in your mind just before going to sleep and knowing the solution in the morning after "sleeping on it". The Universe, to which you are always connected, is given the opportunity of communicating with you in the quiet time when your conscious mind is at rest. This information may or may not be in a dream format. It is, however, still in the nature of dream work.

Programming yourself to remember your dreams is an easy matter and can become a regular part of your emotional healing process. At the close of the day before going to sleep, say to yourself: "Tonight I will dream and remember my dreams and I will be able to correctly interpret them." You can be specific if you wish such as saying: "Tonight I will dream and my dreams will show me the core of some particular problem/limitation with which I am dealing." And, "When I get out of bed in the morning I will have the answers and the new perspective in my mind."

Here, the "first impulse", your intuition, is the one to listen to before the left-brain takes off in some preferred experiential direction that leads you right off track. As has been said before - trust your intuition.

Again, with each individual having their personal dream material, it is impossible to go into analyzing dreams here. You really can do it yourself as long as you believe that you can, and are willing to expend the energy. The results are well worth the effort. Practice makes it much easier and more productive with time.

Chapter 7

RELATIONSHIPS

If you have come immediately to this chapter because a relationship you are having is falling apart, I'm sorry but it won't work. You need the background of the previous information. Go back and get it.

As mentioned in Chapter 1, this book is about changing those aspects of our lives that we find unhappy. While this chapter may seem to be quite gloomy, it should be remembered that it deals with those aspects of relationships we want to change and doesn't talk about the many happy and wondrous relationships we do have. Again, as mentioned in Chapter 1, "Why should we want to change those things that make us happy?" Understanding this, let us proceed with the focus of this chapter, which is dealing with those conditions surrounding relationships we might like to bring into perspective and change.

Relationships are, without a doubt, the most perplexing aspect of life we have to deal with. It is complicated by the fact that we are all different individuals, coming from different experiences and having absorbed life in differing manners. There are many books on relationships that go into detail concerning different aspects of their working that can be referenced; however, we are going to focus on a relatively narrow band of

Change Your Reality

thought. It is the psychological and esoteric reasons concerning the origins of the patterns we see played out, as well as why the relationship happened as it did in the first place.

Keep in mind, that much of the philosophy in this chapter can also be applied to the relationship you have with yourself. In both contexts, there is an interesting sequence of conditions that can be applied to relationships. It is the 4 stages.

1. What's in it for me.
   Totally self-absorbed.
2. Tit for tat.
   You do this and I'll do that makes for equality.
3. I'll do it for the sake of the relationship.
   I'll give up hockey, choir, since you don't like it.
4. One and one is three.
   I am happy with what makes you happy and likewise, However, when we are together, it is magical.

One may be in one stage concerning one subject (money?), while being in another stage regarding something else (leisure time?). Give it a try on some relationships you have, either with yourself, or other people or perhaps other couples.

The intention is that you might understand what you are both doing and possibly make some better-informed choices as to the present and future. Addressing your own stuff will help the situation but it would improve the probabilities of achieving what you envision as a "perfect" relationship if you were both searching for the keys to harmony, joy and happiness - both individually and together. This assumes that it really is the best for both of you that the relationship continues and that you can come from such a mindset.

There is always the chance that you two have completed your learning experiences with each other and it is time to move on. Either way, exploration of the causes and effects of your current situation are worth pursuing.

If your vibrations do diverge, allow that it is a natural progression for both of you, and be at peace with the coming change.

But first, there is something you have to accept as part of your and the other person's growth:

> You cannot assume responsibility for anyone's life, other than your own.

By deciding "for someone else" what their life should be, you are doing three things.

1. Limiting the other person's choices, experiences and growth.
2. Limiting yourself in choosing your potential growth.
3. Limiting the Universe in bringing you both what you consciously choose from the situation you are now in.

"Well", you might say, "what if this interrelationship is what we both chose from the beginning?" Well, you actually did, but is it what you want to continue to choose? The idea here is to achieve perspective about the situation. Have your individual and collective vibrations changed and are you "hanging on" because there is fear in the change? This IS your life. Be aware, conscious, and active in managing it. Take your power from your programming. Be who you want to be. Consciously instruct the Universal machine as to what you want.

One might ask: "What if I change and the other person still wants to fight?" Have you ever heard the sound of one hand clapping? What happens? The person will probably be angry that you won't play the game any more, so they will have to find someone else to provide the "other hand" on whom to vent their anger. And you walk away.

As mentioned previously, the law that runs this place and your life is "Like Vibrations Attract". Within the context of a relationship it is what brings you together, keeps you together and breaks you up. This "vibration" is changing continuously, so to want, or expect, that things don't change once the "right" person comes along is impossible, in addition to not being fair for either of you. The ideal situation might be that your mutual vibrations and the collective vibration of the two of you continues to change in harmony. This person may be in your life for a short or long time depending on the potential and desire for growth. Cosmically it doesn't make any difference because in the greater scheme of things, once love has been shared, it is forever. For most reading this book, any relationship, be it friend or lover, may have deep roots in other lives. It is the nature of existence to share experiences on the upward movement of change.

Consciousness is forever.

The beingness of a relationship is also deeply rooted in our genetic makeup. As a species we will not exist unless we procreate. This literally drives us into relationships when logic often says: "Forget it". In the animal world we find ourselves "falling in love" at an early age. These awakened drives insure that the species is continued from young and viable stock. Although some will disagree, our sexuality generally peaks from puberty into the early 20's, when it seems almost too much to handle. After that, it becomes habitual and recreational and not driven so much by species-needs. It can be potentially much more fun. But then there is compulsive sex. The source of that behavior is a rich vein to explore.

One of the most puzzling aspects of falling in love is the behavior patterns we display when this first happens. The very <u>FIRST</u> time this happens, we find ourselves walking around behind the person and wanting to be with them no matter what they are doing or where they are going. We "miss" them if they leave the room and if they go away for any extended period of time, it results in "madness" (or so it seems). We want to be touched by them all the time and so on. There is a good reason for this. It is the first time the intense feelings of literally being one and totally belonging are brought up since the relationship with mother as an infant. These feelings are a perfect duplication of that period of time in our lives. They make us REALLY want to make babies. The ritual of being "carried" across the threshold is wanting to be "carried" by mother again into that most sacred and safest of places. It harkens back to before we had a concept of time or that there even was a separation between you and mother.

The next logical step, assuming you lived through that experience, was to fall "out of love". Well, this raises intense feelings of abandonment, loneliness, powerlessness, ineptitude and being not only unloved but also unlovable - by anyone. It is an extremely intense time; for these are the same feelings you had when mother "left" you to go get dinner. The issue is survival. Part of you has been removed and it is the essential part that provides you with your needs. Without that "part", you cannot survive.

Please note - only from a child's mind will this be the reaction. It brings up the old black and white absoluteness of a child's reasoning again.

When a relationship is failing and we argue, we are coming from a distinct posture of "survival". There is no logic involved at all; it is a very real matter of "life and death" and totally emotional. A person is "in the corner" and fighting for their life. The arguments are extremely hurtful and come from that "survival" place but also come from another genetically driven response.

What is added to the energy of the survival response is the defense response. It is manifest through the desire to hurt someone who has hurt you deeply.

What a person is really doing in this case is demonstrating just how hurt they are. One of the most prevalent responses to this situation comes from childhood where someone has hurt you and you want to hurt them back. BIG TIME!! The "victim" is also demonstrating their total feelings of powerlessness, ineptitude and feeling unloved. It is no wonder that their world seems to be "crashing down around their heads." Their physical world is unraveling, their emotional world is in a tailspin and their mental world is in a total state of confusion.

Deciding to terminate a relationship raises significant survival responses. Our feelings are that we must stay together at any cost. We feel that this is safer than nothing and nothing is what we will have if we leave. There isn't a chance that we will find anyone who will have anything to do with us (regardless that the entire human race is out there and changing too). In addition, there is the potential problem of children. All of a sudden, we will put up with anything, and do, until the pain becomes great enough to force change. Then we have to go through the emotional tearing apart and the mourning associated with change. Major YUK.

We are also responding to many of the deep-seated survival patterns from our genetic pool. All of these genes drive us to stay where we are unto death or at least until the family grows up.

In addition to this are the many beliefs instilled in us by society and our religions about the sanctity, obligation and "until death do us part" requirements we have accepted regarding our "contract".

The first time this happens is the worst, in both the loving and leaving modes. The second and later times the experience is understood to a degree, has been dealt with before, and has some perspective surrounding it. It still hurts but you aren't quite on automatic to the same degree. The time after that it is some better and so on. Maturity, through experience, often makes the "second time around" much more fulfilling and wonderful. But it also makes totally giving of your self, doubtful. There is an underlying protection mode operating in the background "just in case".

Some never recover from the first time. They are hurt so badly that such behavior is banned from their future experiential allowing. But genetics comes into play again and the need to preserve the species (having a potential greater than preservation of the individual) sends most people out into the fray for a second try. Even so, they are much more cautious about opening their hearts and have essentially become love/intimacy-shy.

Fear of intimacy is one of the most powerful resistances we create and one of the most limiting behavior patterns for having wonderful relationships. The primary causal event in being afraid of becoming intimate is the loss of intimacy with mother. The next on the list is loss of intimacy with your first love. Another potential source is where a child is taken away from his intimate friends without sufficient preparation. Intimacy is the deepest emotional involvement we have with another, and therefore the most sensitive. Consequently it hurts the most when denied, and we feel abandoned at the core of our emotional being. Realization of the source, the effect and the genetic nature of the problem can help us to bring the situation into perspective. Finding the causal events and releasing the emotional blockages can help in being able to again feel the tenderness of intimacy. It was all experience, and you were not abandoned. Everyone involved was simply living their lives as they might, as were you.

As a potential release of the trauma associated with these events, the "De-energizing Technique" given in Chapter 4 can be helpful.

The fear of opening yourself up to another and loving them totally is also common. This stems from the same source of experiences. Perhaps keeping in mind that each experience of love allows one to expand into a greater capacity to love and, if you want it, allow the Universe to bring you another opportunity to love and learn.

Knowing that there will always be someone out there to share life with, if you still desire to have a relationship, can help free yourself to experience the best a relationship has to offer. As you may recall, one of my "druthers" (Chapter 3) is a "Perfect interrelationship on the physical, emotional, mental and spiritual levels." This is an instruction to the Universal computer.

Surviving the breakup of a deep love affair is certainly traumatic, but it is not the end. Compromising and remaining in the relationship because "I am too old now, and this is my last chance", is a statement of lack of self-love and worth, as well as perspective. When you truly love yourself, you know without question that your vibration will attract to you someone of your level of beingness at an appropriate time. Sometimes patience is called for while each of you ready yourselves for this wonderful new experience. In this state of mind you think that if someone doesn't find you "irresistible" it is their problem, not yours. And it is.

All too often, at a surface or subliminal level, we think of a relationship that is breaking up as a failure. It is never this and thoughts in this mode are only self-destructive. Failure is not possible, only change for all involved.

<u>It is all just experience.</u>

As you and your partner travel individual rivers of life, it is only natural that sometimes the rivers diverge in their flow. You change, the partner changes, and that's all there is to it. True, the emotional trauma may be severe but that does not change the naturalness of the event. Nor does it preclude another "more wonderful" relationship in the future.

As you may have experienced, there is another factor that can play into finding a new relationship. Energetically the old one must truly be released before a new one can manifest.

Here I would like to list a few of the core beliefs that might limit a new relationship. There can obviously be more. It is up to you to determine whether any of these are valid for you and if there are more hiding in your mind. It is worthwhile as you read the list to emotionally understand that each of these is only valid because you make it so. It is an excuse, not a truth. Perhaps you really don't want a relationship because you are afraid. I shall also list some potential fears that can limit the potential of a new relationship.

Potential core beliefs for not having a relationship:

I am too old.
Life has passed me by.
Who would want me?
I am damaged goods.
I am too:
  Heavy
  Light
  Eclectic
  Odd
  Weird
  Different

Some potential reasons for being afraid:
There is too much compromise that has to be made.
I am afraid of being hurt again.
Intimacy frightens me.
It is so much work.
I don't want to "settle".
I like being single (this may be true or an excuse, depends).
I don't want to change.

For the above lists, fear is the driving force, because at the level that counts, you know a "perfect" relationship would be synergistic with all of who and what you are, not requiring any of the above and certainly not being "work".

As for the core beliefs, they are a fiction perpetrated upon your self by yourself. They, too, may be excuses and come from fear. All of these can be addressed and put into perspective and released. You now have the tools, the primary one being "The Circle of Experience".

OK - So, you have experience with relationships - no? You fall in love and it feels real good. You have fights and maybe fall out of love and it feels bad. You come up with a series of beliefs as a result which say certain things such as "I want this" or "I want that" or "I DON'T want this", etc. Then, after the next one that also "fails" you come to believe that relationships just aren't for you because you are too:

SOMETHING

Like:

Picky
Old
Odd
Ugly

Beautiful
Hairy
Good
Bad
Emotionally unstable
Emotionally stable
Unfit (whatever that is)

and on and on
and

ON

OR:

"Now I know what I want. They must:
Be interested in music.
Rock
Rap
Glenn Miller
Cook.
Like the out-of doors.
Hate the out-of doors.
Have facial hair.
Have big/small boobs.
Have nice in-laws.
Be my age.
younger.
older.
Be more aggressive.
Be more passive.
Not watch TV news.
Love watching the news every moment."

We could obviously go on and on with the myriad of characteristics the "perfect" relationship will have next time.

Unfortunately you really do not know what a "Perfect" relationship is for you. The Universe does. So how about this:

> "Universe, I want a Perfect relationship and
> I don't have a clue what that means.
> I leave it to you."
> Thanks.

The word forgiveness is often used when releasing internal conflicts with another. Within the perspective of this work, it is an inappropriate term. It assumes that the other person did something wrong. The other person did nothing wrong, no more than you did. The other person, be it parent, lover, ex-spouse or impersonal acquaintance was simply being who they were and expressing behavior patterns developed as a result of their environment. They had no more control over themselves than you do. Oh, so you have complete control and it is all their fault? You fail to realize that YOU created this situation as well as they did and are therefore "at fault" as much as they are.

Remember this:

> There is no such thing as a
> "waste of time".
> All experience has value.

Even though the situation may be uncomfortable in the extreme, still everyone involved is acting out the scenarios of life that were programmed into them over their lives. No blame, only release through understanding the mechanisms that drove the circumstances. In this vein, one can see those who have "wronged" us as whole again - their being as much a mixture of light and dark as are we.

If you keep these mechanisms in mind as you go through the human experience, you may find it easier to be transparent to them and move on through them, realizing that you are mostly responding to your genes and fear-and-survival mechanisms, not your heart. Remember that you are not alone in the world. As before: we are all changing together.

Relationships between friends, neighbors, family and such are just as susceptible to genetic responses as any other. When a person sees a situation subliminally that is a threat to their being or territory, the automatic response will always be in favor of their survival. The responses of fight, flight or freeze will come forth and no reason can be applied to solving the problem. It is for this reason negotiators have to walk a thin(k) line between adversaries.

Emotional responses simply cannot be responded to by intellectual reasoning. Even though someone may have learned to appear calm in such situations, they are still coming from an emotional place and there is nothing that can be productively done until they return to reason. Don't hold your breath. Negotiations are usually performed between "children", each needing to have their own way. The negotiator needs to remove the feelings of being unsafe from the participants before meaningful work can be accomplished. This can be done by personal work but often requires a non-involved counselor.

Often the core issue in relationship problems is trust. You have high expectations of another person and they do something small or large to show you they cannot be trusted. So you begin to look for more reasons to mistrust and LO! There they are. This continues to a point where there is almost no trust and the relationship is in jeopardy. Know this. <u>You trust no one totally because you don't trust yourself.</u> You have seldom, if ever, fulfilled your own expectations of your own performance. How can you expect to trust anyone else?

Answer: You can't.

And don't.

What does this tell you? It tells you that you have work to do on why you don't trust yourself. (We've all had numerous experiences where we "failed" our own expectations). To accomplish this you MUST come from the place that you have always done the best you could with what you had and it was invariably the response of programming. Must, MUST.

Here are some hard ones:

>You can't "fix" anyone else because they are NOT broken. They are Simply being themselves - and doing a Perfect job of it!

>To be "fixed", someone has to realize they are "broken" and WANT to change.

>It is YOU who perceives them as needing to be "fixed".

>Chances are really good they do not agree with you at all, and if asked, they probably think YOU are the one needing to be "fixed".

Relationships, both with partners and the rest of the world are one of our greatest teachers. Keep in mind that the emotional stimuli from seemingly disharmonious circumstances are an integral part of the path each of us has chosen to become the person we have always wanted to be. Becoming that person is the reason you are reading this.

Chapter 8

MANIFESTING DIS-EASE PHYSICALLY

One of the most powerful keys to identifying programs that might be worth changing is the manifesting of our emotional unhappiness physically. Disease is just that: dis-ease with some aspect of our life. That it manifests physically (the <u>emotional</u> dis-ease always comes first) is due to the energy that the emotional disease creates from which the law of "Like Vibrations Attract" manifests into our physicality. Dis-ease is not the direct result of conscious or non-conscious thought that is in our mind, there is a sequence.

The sequence is:

One is feeling dis-ease emotionally about something.

That energy creates, through "Like Vibrations Attract", the manifestation in the physical body.

A couple of thoughts on the matter:
Healing is done in two phases.

First is dealing with the symptoms using either traditional or homeopathic medicines.

Second is addressing and removing the initiating energy that brought it about in the first place.

Sometimes dealing with the second will eliminate the symptoms. Do both in tandem. Some ideas on the matter:

1. No healing is done except by the person being healed. Anyone or anything else involved is a facilitator. This includes doctors and drugs as well as "healers".
2. It is appropriate to ask permission before working with others.
3. There is nothing that is not an integral part of the Whole. This includes doctors, pills and medical procedures. The fact that these opportunities are available as part of the Universe is because it is the only way some people can be healed at this time.
4. Dis-ease in early childhood, or a genetic predisposition to it, is not necessarily a manifestation of emotional conditions. There can be many reasons why a child would choose to come in to be sick or maimed or die of SIDS. When we go into the subject of other lives (Chapter 9), these predispositions and choices will be discussed.
5. You need to be at peace with whatever capabilities you have to self heal. This seeming limitation is a natural and necessary part of evolving.

In this chapter I shall give a general outline of how to find out the emotional cause of the physical ailment. In other words, one goes backwards from the manifesting problem to the cause.

Because we grow up using words to describe our world, the key to understanding what you are "saying" through the dis-ease connects, via words and feelings, to the emotional cause. For instance:

A cold, which causes runny eyes, nose and such, shows the same symptoms as crying. In fact, a cold IS crying on the inside (emotionally) about something with which we are not being honest with ourselves on the "outside". It can also occur simply because the emotional unhappiness is so intense that you need to express it in a powerful manner. The "cold germs" are always available in the body to be activated by such a need of expression and release. Denial of the real emotional responses to life creates energy blockages that can reside in the emotional body until they are released.

At the same time, a seasonal allergic reaction causing runny nose and sneezing may not have a psychological component. But in the search for causes, perhaps the belief that you always have allergies in some season may be released by breaking the "Circle of Experience". It is worthwhile to investigate all possibilities for resulting diseases.

Naturally you don't have to believe this particular aspect to be able to make yourself well, but as a friend of mine once said:

"Good thing the grass doesn't need your permission to grow."

What was being said is that if something works and you don't believe it, it doesn't mean it doesn't work that way, it simply means that you don't accept that it does. And it will continue to work, regardless of your insisted ignorance. Experience with the removal of certain dis-eases by you, will, in very short order, convince you that this is indeed how it works.

So what about the placebo effect? That is why "snake oil" and product endorsements indicate a product works for some and may not work for you at all. In scientific tests, the FDA may find no correlation between apricot seeds and the healing of cancerous conditions, but that doesn't mean it doesn't work for someone who really believes it does. The difference is in the power of the mind that is not taken into account in clinical studies. In simple terms it is our beliefs that most significantly govern the effectiveness of any treatment.

It is appropriate here to again mention a pivotal point in working with others as a "healer".

No healing is done
except by the person being healed.
All healers are catalysts and conduits for this purpose.

There is a point at which a person decides they CAN be healed. In that moment, they may decide that a "healer" will make it possible. The Universe will bring to them that "healer". It is the person being healed who "allows" the healer to do their job because they expect it to work. Among other things, this perspective keeps the ego in check.

In like manner, those who do not believe that healing can occur, for any reason, can call forth the most powerful healer and nothing will happen. This is true for medications as well. "Antibiotics don't work for me" will insure that this is so.

The Sufi philosophy speaks of miraculous healing as magic that can be likened to the raising of energy levels in electrons surrounding an atom to the next highest orbit/ring. This is how a firefly works. It applies friction to its abdomen and excites the electrons to the next highest energy level (ring of the atom) producing heat through friction. When it stops, the atoms cool and the electrons return to the lower level and give off a photon, which we see as light.

Healing of a miraculous nature can be achieved through this level of energy change of the body. Again, according to the Sufis, this result (achieving magic) can be reached through one of three stimuli: personal power, hate and love. This level of energy is used in many non-traditional communities to create magic. In reality, though, if one knows the physical reason why something works, it is no longer magic, is it?

Thus "miraculous " healing isn't really "magic", its just our ignorance of how it works that gives it that title. Science is always playing "catch-up". There is always a physical explanation for "miraculous" occurrences. It sometimes just takes a broader understanding of how things work, or two millennium of scientific "advancement", to explain the healing "logically".

Another very important aspect of this approach is to keep in mind that sometimes the emotional components are deeply rooted and may have several root causes. Even when the emotional source of the disease is eliminated, it will take the body time to "catch up". The reason to search for the cause/causes is to prevent the disease from returning. As mentioned above, the first item to deal with if a disease manifests, is do what is medically appropriate and THEN look for the "cause".

To "believe" at the surface that you can heal yourself, when non-consciously you don't believe it, will preclude your actually being healed. It might even backfire, meaning that if you believe you are not "good enough" to be healed by alternative methods, your attempt to override your deep programming may cause a negative, instead of a positive reaction. This is totally personal. It requires awareness of yourself in the present.

It is <u>extremely</u> important that you not blame yourself for anything. If you ARE manifesting dis-ease physically, you are being human and rather than come down on yourself, be loving and patient in the search to achieve change. Along this road of what is important, you must keep in mind that there are exceptions.

As just mentioned, those diseases that are genetically programmed, or a result of birth, are not the purview of your emotional creation and to search for "what have you done wrong to deserve this" is not an appropriate posture. There are deeper reasons why you chose these conditions in which to progress through life. Some of the philosophy behind these pre-programmed difficulties is explained in Chapter 9.

You have done nothing wrong in this life or any other. We all are dealing from where we are now and it is from this point that we can choose to change. There is NO other point in which we have any power.

> We can change the past - we can change the probable future, but we can only do it in the NOW.

In my case, the tendency towards rheumatic fever inherited from my grandfather was hardly the emotional creation of an 18-month-old child. It affected me significantly in all aspects of my life and created much unhappiness in the process. However, in retrospect, it was the greatest single gift of my life. It may take time to understand the "gift" of any difficult or life-changing event, but the attitude that it is, and was, a gift is imperative to the process of healing.

This next concept of left brain and right brain reactions to life can be somewhat confusing at times because of the physiology of the human. Brain connections to the body are reversed as they come down into the lower body. That is to say, the left brain, the "thinking "side, manifests on the right side of the body. In like manner the right side of the brain operates the left side of the body. It is important to remember this concerning the subject matter discussed in this chapter.

Whether the malady shows up on the left or right side can tell you more about the emotional source of the disease. For the <u>body</u>, the right side is the male side and is the active, wanting-to-achieve side. The left side is the female or intuitional, philosophical, creative and/or spiritual side. If the right elbow is hurting you feel you do not have the flexibility to reach out and get the "things" or take the actions you want.

If it is the left elbow, you have trouble with reaching out and dealing intuitively, philosophically or spiritually with your world. Again, use your mind to determine what is going on. This is all meant as a guide, it is not absolute or "all or nothing". Just because it doesn't make sense to you now, think on it, and it most likely will. And here's the out. If it doesn't work for you, forget it. The grass will continue to grow.

There is yet another point to consider. If it is your left or right elbow that is hurting are you "saying":

You "want" to move
OR
You "don't want" to move?

Which is it? Movement or non-movement? The elbow is only manifesting your vibration. You have to think about all this to get the answers you seek.

You might want to move through this chapter slowly. Reread it a couple of times to get in the "flow" and see how it "feels".

How about the natural process of aging? What about it? Every incident here must be put in the perspective of the person involved and their current conditions. Is it possible to stop or reverse the natural aging process? Other than the plethora of drugs which do this, I believe the mind indeed has the power to accomplish this through a number of viable physical possibilities. However, the clarity of the vibration is vital and the hundreds of natural blockages from experience and learning may well say "no".

There is a fun and useful exercise that you might want to try.

Stand in front of a mirror with your eyes open and look at yourself. This can be done with or without clothes, full length or partial image. Close your eyes and image yourself looking back at you from the mirror however you would like to look. You could look 30 years younger, or have different body proportions. Perhaps a picture of yourself at some age would be a good place to start. Now imagine that this "image" of yourself is actually you, looking into the mirror from where you are and reflecting your desired physical image. Dwell on it, enjoy it. You may find yourself smiling at the thought. Then open your eyes and go about your business. What you have done is create a thought form. A physical-etheric template that now lays over you and "instructs" your body as it replaces cells with new cells. It is a new blueprint for your physicality.

Do it as often as you like. It can be done with any size mirror once you get the hang of it. After a while you will be able to "image" yourself in this new body while doing any activity. You are programming a "new" physical you.

Achieving results will obviously take time and you may not notice any results for a while. Remember physiological changes are slow, so keep the faith. It IS working.

So, with that under our belts, let's take a look at some of the diseases and their potential emotional cause. It is important to note that these may vary for you and definitely will in certain instances. The reason is that your word concepts will vary from another's. But once the idea is presented, you can go off on your own and make your personal list.

To the list.

It is NOT intended that this list be an absolute list or that there is "something wrong with you emotionally" in any instance. You have to take your own power and THINK. Use your mind and your heart. They are gifts.

Now for some diseases and possible word-associations:

Note: Remember whether it is on the left or right side adds additional clues. Does wanting to change or not wanting to change pertain? Keep in mind also the potential "natural" reactions that may be in play, such as allergies. You have to make this search your own!

Head:	Headed in the wrong direction.
	Needing to knock sense into your head.
Scalp:	Itching to know.
Headache:	Things are not going right.
	Makes my head ache.
Face:	Can't face life.
	Irritated with facing something.
Eyes:	Can't bear to see or watch something.
	Can't see your self doing something.
	Can't see where you're going.
	(unknown future?)
	Can't see clearly (near/far or both)
Ears:	Don't want to hear something.
	left - don't want to hear spiritual stuff.
	right - don't want to hear about reality.
	both - don't want to hear anything.
Pimples:	Can't face situations/irritations of life.
Nose:	Nosing around in other's business.
	Nose to the grindstone.
Sore throat:	Can't speak/scream out.
Tongue:	Not speaking your truth.
Teeth:	Can't get your teeth into something.
	Love, lack of (explained below).
Cold, runny nose:	Crying internally over something.
Fever:	Just burns me up.
Neck:	Something is a "pain in the neck".
Shoulders:	Shouldering uncomfortable responsibility.
	Shouldering one's way into a situation.

Arms:	Left or Right? Can not lift the load. (left or right?)
Elbows:	Inflexibility of reaching out and getting what you want. OR Locking up so there is no change. Keeping from getting something on purpose. Left or Right?
Wrists:	Inflexibility again. Go or no go? Left or right?
Hands:	Inflexibility, inability to grasp what you want.? Again, go or no go? Is it left or right?
Arthritis:	Fixed and rigid in outlook. Fear of moving forward, backwards, or at all. Again, Which side? Beliefs concerning aging can be significant here.
Back:	Supporting too much. Heavy burden of responsibility. Get (the monkey) off my back.
Chest:	Can't get it off my chest. Feel suffocated by circumstances.
Congestion:	Suffocated by something.
Heart:	Broken heart. Heart isn't in it. Don't have the heart (to live?).
Breasts:	My children don't need me. My sexuality is over. I am unattractive.

	I don't want sex anymore.
Allergies:	What are you allergic to?
	Life?
Stomach:	I can't stomach something.
Anal problems:	Can't let go and flow.
	Wanting/deserving to be screwed.
	Wanting to get rid of stuff.
	Wanting to be cared for as a baby again.
Constipation:	Keeping everything in.
	Fear of letting it all out.
Diarrhea:	Wanting to get rid of something, real bad - NOW!
Intestinal:	Can't "digest"- deal with - life.
Solar plexus:	The seat of emotional turmoil.
Rear end:	Something is a pain in the ass.
Anal leakage:	Want to get rid of the stuff.
	Want to be loved as a baby again.
Incontinence:	Having no control.
	Wanting to be loved as a baby again.
Prostate:	I am no longer sexy.
Legs:	No power to move any more.
	Left or right.
Knees:	Inflexibility in moving forward.
	Failing to bow to the spirit within you.
	Left or Right is important.
Ankles:	Inflexibility for moving forward.
	Again, left or right is important.
Feet:	Can't "stand" something.
	Don't understand.
	Lacking direction.
	Doing too much (moving).
	Left or Right?
	Lacking spiritual direction.
Toes:	Balance.

Change Your Reality

Fever:	Really 'hot' about something.
Skin irritations:	Generally irritated, location will tell you where - could it be totally? Irritated about everything!
Gall Bladder:	Not having the "gall" to deal.
Nerves:	Not having the nerve (associated with where). Being "nervous" about something. Where it is will help.
Weight:	Protection against life's unhappiness. Desire to keep baby fat to stay "helpless". Wanting to be unattractive to avoid emotional hurt.
Cancer:	Uncontrolled emotionality, Location will tell you what.

The reason teeth are love is because it is with this part of our bodies that we suckle at mother's breast. True, at that time we had no teeth, but use this concept and you may find a path.

Cancer is the uncontrolled fear associated with the organ involved. Internal organs are keeping things in. It can also be the desire to die.

Do you notice the word association in these cases and can you see why your words may mean something different? This is important to remember. Most of these reactions will be due to a learned response. You need to be aware and present to make this information useful.

Accepting the "truth" of this approach is entirely up to you. You can't do it wrong. There are no requirements that you process your life in any manner other than that which you choose. If you do choose to allow for the concept to be partially true, then allow that. It is all choice.

What did I leave out in the list above? Not much, only about a couple of thousand pages from the AMA medical dictionary, and the way you think about things, that's all. You will have to do the work for yourself. This is only a guide, if it was meant to be a definitive dissertation, it would be 4 million pages long and you wouldn't even BEGIN to look at it.

This can not be said enough times; none of these are absolute. If you lift weights and have a lactic acid burn from working out, this is obviously not a manifestation of dis-ease: it is a natural reaction to the working of your body. Likewise tennis elbow. . . but wait! Is it ONLY the exercise? Don't go to someone else to find out "what you are manifesting," only you know the answers. The first question to ask is:

"Is there an emotional component to this problem?"

The next item to deal with is what do you do with this information? You take the statement you feel associates your emotional dis-ease and work with it to eliminate it as shown in the other chapters of the book.

Let's take an example. Use either the pendulum or kinesiology tool.

Statement: My back hurts.

Q: Is there an emotional component?

A: (most likely) Yes.

Q: What do I believe that my back hurts?

A: I am manifesting "my aching back" because I feel/believe I am overwhelmed with responsibilities concerning work, family, moving forward, friends, and whatever might be the case.

Q: Then I believe that I cannot handle this situation to my/others level of expectation?

A: Yes.

Q: Is this necessarily true? Is everything about this situation beyond my ability to cope?

A: No, only parts.

Q: Which parts?

A: These and those parts.

Q: Do I really believe I cannot cope with the situation if I break it up into smaller pieces?
A: No. If the pieces are small enough, I can deal with it.
Q: So do I still feel I am totally overwhelmed with the situation?
A: No. Not totally.
Q: So do I still have emotional dis-ease with the situation?
A: Hopefully not, we'll see now, won't we?
Q: Is there any physical damage that cannot be healed now?
A: No.

If "yes" then appropriate actions and time will have to be taken to allow for the physical repair.

Pay attention to the back and see if the pain does not lessen or go away. If it does not, then you would ask why? Is there something else? The answer might well be yes and you would ask what? You would then go into the search mode again until you felt both emotionally and physically that you've got it. The answer may be "no" but the back continues to hurt. It may simply be that the back needs time to rebalance/heal. You may also need to go see a specialist. THINK.

There is an experience I would like to share here. I call it the "Fat Tongue Experience".

I had been working at a friend's for a couple of weeks with a "high conflict" personality. That means that there are no right answers and whatever you say the other person must have a response. I was learning not to respond to the jibes pretty well when, after several days I saw that my tongue was swelling. At first I thought it was something in my diet, but it become bad enough, with nothing working, that I finally asked if there was a psychological component to the situation. "Yes" was the answer. Following the lead that it was potentially about speaking, I came up with "I was not speaking my truth". Of course doing so would have been a poor choice to maintain peace, so I addressed this and within a couple of hours, the tongue went back to normal. Sometimes we subliminally cannot have the perspective desired and that is OK. We're still doing the best we can with what we have.

In a situation such as this, you might speak to your inner self and explain that you accept the fact that you are not "speaking your truth", and it is OK. The reason for this is it would not be particularly good for anyone involved. At a conscious level we are now comfortable enough to just let it be.

If, as in another example, you might say of yourself that you are acting like a baby, you might well find yourself physically acting like a baby - such as being incontinent with loose stool and no control. Certainly a baby-like action.

The same can be said for calling yourself immature. In order to make yourself "right", you may find yourself acting immature at times when this is totally inappropriate. You are just manifesting your beliefs and your truths as to what you are.

In Native American healing practices there is a saying that while the energy may have brought healing, it may take a little while for the body to catch up.

The primary key to finding the emotional source of the dis-ease is to ask the question:

"What do I believe that this is the case?"

Please note this, because it should be your first step in pursuing the emotional causes.

There has been much said about making positive statements to make one's life better. This approach creates a vibration that does indeed affect your reality. It is especially true in working with the body. Continuing to say "I feel tired" sends an internal message to the body that definitely has an effect. Statements, in this case, which would seem counter to the obvious situation might be:

Change Your Reality

"My body can rest and refresh itself. I can take a few moments to stop, take a couple of deep breaths, and allow my body to begin the healing process."

It is a change of attitude and consciousness to realize you CAN make a difference. It also changes your vibration towards healing. You have to start with the belief that you can, AND not reinforce the feeling of tiredness. Yes, it might take some time, but the situation needs a point at which you consciously turn it around and provide a new direction.

One of the most effective tools I have used is to talk to the body. There are about 37 trillion cells in your body. While they work together with each other, there is no "conscious coordinator". You can be that. The first time you address the body is much like a voice out of the heavens talking to a mass of people. They hear it and go "Oooh, it must be God - we better listen". In the following statement I use, I specifically use the 37 trillion number because it is an unimaginably large number and confirms that ALL of us are working together. This is a really BIG team! It goes like this:

"Hey body, listen up! All thirty seven trillion of us give our self permission to heal this situation now. Let's get on with it!!"

Then I might go to the pendulum and ask the body if there is any problem with getting on with the physical healing. If there is, then back to find the belief that continues to drive the dis-ease.

This would come after I have identified that there WAS a dis-ease emotionally, and dealt with it. And now comes the physical part - healing the body.

Depending on the situation, a follow-on statement might be worthwhile such as:

"We might have dis-ease with something, but there is no need to manifest it physically. We know what is going on and are working on it, so let's get on with the healing."

You ARE the creator of your physical reality so act like it!

In some situations, there may well be a continuing of the emotional dis-ease and you really want to "cry". Then do it - the emotional reaction is honesty being manifested and released.

It is also common to have the same situations come up again and again, even after you thought you had dealt with it. Why? Because the emotional stimulus for being unhappy still resides within your psyche. That's totally OK, just be consistent and persistent in your work. You are reprogramming years of the same reactions and perspectives. Patience.

This is a system that has had remarkable effects for some people, but one needs to use it, not just intellectualize it. See what it can do for you. As in all this work the beliefs you have regarding your own ability to heal yourself will play.

As a friend once said "The child constantly needs to be attended to." What this says, as in a situation where muscles in your physical body want to return to the old pattern after a chiropractic adjustment, is that behavior patterns do not necessarily go away on the first try. You need to stay aware of what you are doing. Keep at it and eventually the new/desired pattern will become the norm. It's called reprogramming.

You CAN significantly effect your physiology. To what degree? That is up to you. Where does mind control end and magic begin? Find out for yourself.

The first step is to believe it is possible. The second step is to ask yourself what beliefs you have that it is not, or what limitations you believe exist outside your own beingness.

As a point of interest, have you ever wondered why someone who has "done everything right" and always eaten healthy dies young? Could it be that they are eating "right" out of fear of dying and create that reality rather than eating "right" out of love and respect for their body and the gift of life.

Always check out your beliefs

in regard to any regimen
you embrace.

A worthwhile book for additional information on this matter is *Who's The Matter With Me* by Alice Steadman. A second book that goes into more detail concerning the mechanics of the process is Jane Robert's *The Nature of Personal Reality*.

So now, where are you in relation to the idea of manifesting disease physically? For some it is a bit much. Especially when dealing with major diseases such as cancer. This is totally OK. Believe at the level you choose, but don't throw out the baby with the bathwater. Allow that at least SOME of your diseases are manifestations of emotional dis-ease and work with those.

Once again, everything shared here is my philosophy based on my experiences and may not be yours. Take what feels right and forget the rest. As you continue in the self-work you will arrive at your own philosophical place.

Chapter 9

THE REST OF THE STORY

The chapter is called "The Rest of the Story" because there is an additional component to the existence of each of us that is not physical and because there is much more to our "history" than is obvious. Some of the more esoteric aspects of our lives are covered here including those referred to as "will be explained in Chapter 9" in previous chapters.

It is worth saying again that the information in this chapter is NOT necessary to make the simple "I Choose to BE Happy" approach work to changing your reality. If this information is not comfortable for you, then ignore it. I share my truth, but it does not have to, nor need to be, yours.

"Like Vibrations Attract" works in the non-physical Universe as well as the physical. In the chapter on dreams, it is mentioned that Jungian philosophy draws on the non-physical, the "Collective Unconscious", for creation and interpretation of some dreams. It is reported that 85% of the population believes in some sort of afterlife awareness. A quote of many spiritual seekers is:

"We are much more
than our physical bodies."

The rest of the chapter is sharing with you some concepts in this regard.

One of the primary concepts is that of there being a sequence of experiences called "other lives". Other lives are not lived in sequence and are not necessarily in the past. They can just as easily be in the "future", for there is no past nor future, there is only the Now on the other side of the veil. Nonetheless, other lives are real and coexisting with you in this eternal now. Their representative in the present is carried in the DNA in all 37 trillion cells of your body. This fact leads to the concept of "cellular memory". It is possible to connect with these lives if you choose. A technique called "The Cocoon" is presented later as one possibility for doing this. Richard Bach, in *Illusions*, uses movies as a metaphor wherein you can go into a theater and see any movie (life) of your choice. An important reference concerning the multi-dimensional nature of DNA is discussed in Kryon Book 12, *The 12 Layers of DNA*.

Many compulsive behaviors in this life are based upon experiences in other lives and manifest as very real current patterns. Thus, when addressing these behaviors, it may well be worthwhile to ascertain the source of these. Some of the primary lessons to be learned in this life may indeed be to move beyond those programming limitations carried forward in your DNA. The Cocoon exercise is a potential tool for doing this on your own or with someone else. It can also be done by contacting a person who is versed in the practice of assisting one to look into other lives. The technique is called "past life regression".

DNA is not intelligent in it's own right. It is a memory bank of what went on "before" and a set of instructions, both physical and non-physical, that guide your response to life on many levels. It contains the potential for change through your change in vibrational frequency. This "potential" can be exercised through conscious awareness.

For those who do not know whether there are other lives or not, I offer an exercise and some examples to tickle your imagination. The exercise is to look at your current behavior patterns, likes and dislikes and "knowings" and ascertain whether there are any that can not be explained by your upbringing. Some potential examples:

You've always been fascinated by some place that you or your family have never visited.

You have some "talent" that has no explanation in your current history.

You find yourself feeling "you've been here before" when you know you haven't (dejavu).

You find yourself loving some venue that you haven't been exposed to, such as opera or jousting.

You find yourself standing in a ballet posture at a water fountain when you never took ballet.

You have a totally unreasoning fear of heights, water, fish or some animals.

You find you can play a certain instrument as if you always have.

You get pictures of situations with other people that just pop up and seem to have no now-time context (sitting on a horse, in some costume).

The "rememberings" carried by the cellular memory are an integral part of every cell contained in your multi-layer DNA. Knowing the mechanics of how it works and the problems in releasing this programming can be useful in achieving your goals.

The total DNA is present from the very first division of the zygote. Every resulting cell contains the full memories as the cells generate. The memories of other lives begin to become an active part of our operating system as soon as the body reaches a sufficient level of development to respond. The fear components from these lives are thus active immediately upon sufficient maturation in order to help keep us safe from "dangers" drawn from this or other lives. Unfortunately, these fear-causing experiences manifest through the reptilian brain since it is the first part of the brain to develop. This makes these "experiential fears" hardwired and difficult to remove.

The reptilian brain does not respond to "a thinking approach" because it cannot think. To remove these "hardwired" programs it is necessary to address each life and incident individually. Depending on your "history", this may take many work sessions. For some people, the experiences from other lives are inconsequential in this life, and there is nothing significant to address. Even after you have achieved a total merging of your behavior patterns and history in this life, some of these may still be in place. All of this is to say: "Be patient and persistent in your quest", and know that you can not do "it" wrong. You will still get to "go home".

Here I would like to share a personal experience whereby a "past life" experience significantly affected "this life" patterns. It begins with the nature of work that I have done in this life, specifically construction. I did this work primarily as a one-man construction company, doing electrical, plumbing, framing, drywall and pretty much everything else it takes to build. There are two things I noticed during the many years I did this work that were consistent with every job. The first was that with the beginning of each job there was considerable anxiety, seemingly out of proportion to the task required. The second was that I was very nervous about doing plumbing and, as a result, things usually leaked. It turns out that both of these conditions would not relinquish their anxieties through the use of the tools shared in this book. So, I looked into other lives.

"Once upon a time" there was a plumber as part of a team that was tasked to create a large lake for the full size re-creation of important naval battles. It was an artificial lake that had, as an integral part of its construction, the ability to be drained when the show was finished. Somehow, during the show, the lake emptied, leaving the ships high and dry and the emperor really, really unhappy. There needed to be a scapegoat, as there always is for such a disaster, and I was it. Thus I was executed for my "crimes".

What I "remembered" was recorded in my DNA as a very unhappy experience that resulted in a painful death. As a result, I was afraid of plumbing "leaks" and of taking on any job for fear of "paying the ultimate price". It may be fun to think of it now, but only after the release provided by emotionally realizing that it was "just experience" and "so what" could this perspective be achieved.

You might ask how I became aware of this. Here is another tool that you might find helpful. Either this or the "cocoon" can be used. It was introduced in Chapter 4 and is called the "light pictograph".

It was through this internal imaging that the cause of my fears came to mind through setting my intent and asking the question: "What is the source of my problem with plumbing and doing big jobs?" I set my mind to neutral and allowed pictures to form. While this takes practice, it is virtually the same as remembering something that you saw before. Once the basic image is formed, you can ask questions. This is what happened: I first got a picture of the Coliseum in Rome. It was not enough to get any idea of what went on, so I asked "Where am I in this picture?" The focus turned into a picture of it with boats sitting on the internal ground with no water. Still no me, so I asked again. The focus changed to several people running around in a panic somewhere in the arena and the feeling was that they were responding to a disaster. I was among them. "So, what happened next?" I get a picture of someone being crucified. The feeling was very powerful that it was me, and the rest of the story came into focus. I got the blame. Someone had to pay.

Change Your Reality

This is not as difficult as it may seem. It is important that you leave your judgment at home and pursue the desired result. The imaging is similar to the imaging used in the "Active Imagination" exercise in Chapter 6. It is important not to try too hard to get results. Relax and give yourself a chance. If this approach doesn't work for you, the "cocoon" or engaging a person that can do past life regressions may work better.

As mentioned before, not everyone has such traumatic experiences that result in limitations in this life, but one just may. Be open to the possibility and remember, it was all just experience and does not mean that anything like it might ever happen again. It is up to you to sort out the probabilities of being "punished" for some transgression that could not possibility happen in this life. It is not likely that I will be punished by death for having a plumbing repair leak. Plumbing, by the way, is no longer a source of anxiety, nor is a new job. It appears that emotionally accepting the outcome as just another experience and putting it in perspective released the anxiety.

One might ask why would such a specific experience end up with such grand generalities in this life and the answer is because these "memories" become active very early in our life and are judged on the basis of a very simplistic brain functionality. It is only later in life that our minds are developed sufficiently to adequately categorize the true narrowness and pertinence of such an event.

The path to awareness, experienced over many lifetimes, can be likened to the growth of a human in that there are stages of growth that begin with infant and progress through baby, young, mature and old. These are general categories, as they are in humans but have the same general characteristics of that age of growth. "As it is above, so it is below" and the growth of the human over the accumulative lifetimes also mirrors the evolvement in consciousness of the Universal whole. Below is a list and the general personality manifestations shown by each grouping.

You will recognize these characteristics in others, and perhaps judge them accordingly, but remember, can you really feel superior to a 4 year old? You have no idea how they will develop. Over many lives, like you, they will also become magnificent beings of light. Love them on their path as you have come to love you on yours.

Infant: Concerned only with survival. The world revolves around the person at this stage and they are totally self-absorbed and even unaware that there is anyone else. It is said that there are no infant souls in earth at this time of transition.

Baby: Still totally self-absorbed and concerned with survival. There are few people in their world and those involved are there to serve them. All their relationships are stage one - what's in it for me? There is almost no social consciousness at this stage.

Young: Beginning to get interesting. This covers the human age group from the baby years through the forties or so, maybe even for a lifetime. This is the "go get 'em, walk all over everyone, huge amounts of energy stage. They are still very self-absorbed with their "success" and image among peers and the rest of the world. They are likely a social climber, being one who is powerfully motivated by having much stuff and living better and more showy than others. They get involved in causes with significant energy, want big boats, giant homes and have, what appears to others, little depth.

Mature: Done much of it. Conservative. Afraid of losing what "little" they have (which may be anything other than little). Owned by the fear of impending death and live in gated communities to keep themselves safe. Highly regimented because it is safe knowing what comes next. Not very flexible in changing. Frightened of much of life and live an existence in which the allowed experiences become fewer and narrower.

The "causes" (charities) are generally established charities and organizations.

Old: Been there, done that. Experience has given them a varied set of interests. Not terribly concerned with conformity, not terribly afraid to try something new. A little taken aback by the inflexibility and fear of the mature folks and almost totally non-judgmental except on themselves. Often this last barrier (judgment) is a major learning potential for their current life. Old souls will often be sincerely interested in your well being.

Lives are not lived in a timing sequence, for whatever time/space is necessary for the chosen learning experiences will be used. Lives are not sequential - i.e. one life does not end and then another one begin in linear time. Since there is only the Now, linear time is somewhat meaningless in this context.

A detailed explanation of this concept is presented in *The Michael Handbook* by Jose Stevens and Simon Warwick-Smith.

The "tree of life" is a common concept in many religions and philosophies. What follows is a concept of what this term might signify. Think of a pine tree while thinking about the concept.

The "other" aspects of who you are can be likened to belonging to a tree. Each branch growing off the trunk of the tree contains a series of "smaller branches" (called fragments) of which you are one. The entire branch consists of all of the lives you have lead to this moment. You are the culmination of the experiences of each of your other lives on that branch. You are the finger of awareness of the soul expressed in the physical that experiences a series of lives that move along a path from ignorance to enlightenment. There are many branches on a soul's tree. Each branch contains a "Higher Self" as an overseer for that set of experiences. The entire tree, consisting of the many branches is the "Soul" energy from which the higher selves, and you, spring. In short, you are part of an individual branch containing many lives, and a tree that contains many branches.. For an interesting example of how a "higher self" works, you might read Jane Robert's *The Education of Oversoul 7*.

In esoteric circles the term "higher self" and "Soul" are often used interchangeably. They are not the same. The experiences of the "higher self" is limited by the growth on the individual branch and generally is not any more "mature" than you are. The "soul", having the accumulation of experience of many "branches" and being the original source for them, has a higher vibration and accumulated wisdom. For most, the maturity of the "soul" energy over that of the "higher self "is obvious once you become aware of the difference.

There are many questions that arise concerning the concept of other lives. Such as:

Why? Because in order to appropriately be able to choose how you would like to express yourself, you need to experience both sides of many situations. This is what duality is about. You get to be the bad guy and the good guy, tortured and torturer, happy and sad and so forth. As you gather the wisdom of these experiences you become a knowledgeable co-creator with the Universe, capable of deciding how you want to manifest as a point of consciousness.

Earth is not a kindergarten, it is a graduate school containing all the necessary experiences and conditions needed for, and leading to, this graduation.

How many lives? Depends on how fast a learner you are - from several hundred to a couple of thousand. Usually around 800 or so.

How do other lives interact with me as a new human? Primarily through cellular memory which is contained in the multidimensional nature of your DNA. Cellular memory is similar to pouring rum over a cake that is then absorbed throughout. All cells remember, not just the brain. The input arrives when the human is capable of absorbing the information.

It is in the DNA from the start but much of the DNA cannot activate until the human is in the right sequential position. (Similar to puberty not happening until the appropriate age.)

How does this cellular memory interact with me after I grow up? The experiences you had can bring forth capabilities and responses of two different sorts. One is long term in nature (you've played the violin and naturally take it up again, lived in Paris etc. and having loved someone "before") and a short-term event, usually traumatic (such as drowning, falling or dying uncomfortably).

What kinds of things are brought forward into cellular memory other than long and short term effects? A couple of the most important memories brought forward involves vows and/or curses you have taken in previous lives. These can be from the church or to any organization or even from/to your self. (Having had your head cut off for having money, you vow that you will NEVER allow yourself to be rich again). Another significant potential is fear of becoming enlightened because you lost your life in Atlantis, or wherever, and concluded that it was because you were enlightened. Many older souls are naturally afraid of coming out of the cave because they have been severely prosecuted for speaking their truth. It must be noted that at this time in history those fears are no longer valid. Release of these fears can significantly assist in changing a poor self-image.

How do you remove these vows? By saying out loud: "Universe, (Spirit) I release all vows and curses of any kind made under any circumstances NOW. This is permanent".

How do other lives interact with me in the present? Generally, not specifically, except through cellular memory. There is a "bleed through" between you and your other lives as mentioned above, so that what you do affects them some and visa versa.

Do other lives affect me in the present? Yes, but to significantly varying degrees. Again, it depends on the specifics of the life involved. For many it may just be a curiosity.

How can I know whether to pursue other life experiences or not? The choice is yours. Generally situations that have been "set up" to happen in this life are residuals from other lives because you want to address their effects in some way. For many, this includes "Karmic" events that do not need to be "addressed" but can be released through choice as mentioned below. In general one would pursue other lives as a source of a problem only if you had thoroughly dealt with the causes from this life and there seemed to be no resolution. There is a technique, "The Cocoon", which is shared below for looking into other lives. There is also the imaging technique (light pictograph) as well as practitioners who can assist.

Do other lives have the power to run my life? Not unless you let them. You are the point of consciousness in the present and therefore anything "they" try to do can only be done with your permission. Take the position of power by claiming you are the driver and you (other parts) get in the back seat. Enough!

Do you have to deal with other lives specifically if a limitation seems to come from there? Not necessarily. If some belief comes from another life the belief exists in this life through your consciousness and can be released in the present. There is no need to know where or when the belief was created.

How do I know whether a belief comes from another life or not? The source doesn't make any difference. The release is in the present.

Concerning the traumatic events and their carryover, how do I deal with them? Assuming your fear is not this-life based (falling, drowning, being burned, etc.) the situation is more complicated. Asking if you drowned (fell, etc.) in another life may have a picture or feeling associated with it. If this occurs, and the fear can be felt, reaffirm that your intent is to release the event and use the de-energizing technique". This brings perspective to the event in order to reduce the emotional response. It may take some work, but it usually has good results.

What if no good results are achieved? If the resulting fear is not debilitating then just don't go in the water. If it is, see a professional.

Kryon (Kryon.com) has suggested that the human body is actually designed to last 900 years. If this is really the case, then why so short a time span for each life? First, can you imagine living with the problems you have for several hundred years? It's a relief to let them go and move on. Second it allows a large number of very different experiences to "flavor" your attitude and give you choices from which to develop how you want to manifest.

Do we really travel in groups? Generally yes. Each partner in the group-experience plays different roles for purposes of working together to achieve the ultimate goal - awareness/enlightenment. This is why your experiences with those closest to you are so "deep". You will play different parts (son, daughter, mother, boss, lover etc.), as will they, each helping the other to achieve growth as desired. It is also how you gain perspective in relationships of all kinds.

Is it possible to have more than one incarnation in the same time/space? Yes, although they usually do not meet one another during their lifetimes because their goals and stage of soul growth are different. Yet it does happen and I have experienced three people of similar ages who had the same soul energy. They didn't know each other previously to meeting and came from dissimilar backgrounds. Their mannerisms, likes and dislikes and possessions were very similar. There was a powerful affinity between all three.

Can you jump from one level of soul growth to another between lives? Other than the natural progression in which this occurs, "skipping" over a level is not generally possible. The progression is actually linear in a growth sense (not time sense) and decisions as to what you are going to do in the next life are made from the level of experience you have in the one you just left. You are the one making the decisions. Others inform and perhaps recommend, but it is all about YOU, your choices, and your life plan.

Is it possible to transition from this life to the "next" while still in this life? Yes. How? By choice. How would you know whether you had done or are doing this? By a significant change in your attitude that the "old" you would simply not have embraced. By recognizing that there might have been a "null point" where everything went to zero (it seemed) and a truly "new" you seemed to emerge. This is not as uncommon as it might seem. We, as humans, are changing consciousness very rapidly at this time in history.

What about judgment after death? You are the only person who judges yourself. The Universe/God does not judge. You are given free choice as to what you want to do next. There are those with you during this "life review" that are there to help, but you are the one who decides. You might be interested in *Journey of Souls.* by Michael Newton that goes into the period between lives gleaned from work with individuals in his psychiatric practice.

What about Karma? There is no karma except that which is created by you. You decide what relationship you "have to" have with others in conjunction with those individuals. This "Karma" is a "contract" as explained below. It can be voided through conscious choice. Having free choice, you may choose to "pay" for some thing you perceive as a "transgression" in one life in the next. The decision that you "owe" someone something or have to be paid back because of something you did to them is based on the ignorance that the energies were not balanced at the time of the "transgression". These experiences were chosen by both parties, having been created for purposes of mutual growth.

When a person attracts a "good" or "bad" situation to themselves in some life, the other person desires to experience the other side of the experience for their own reasons. The energy expended is equal and proper at the time of the occurrence and needs no other action to be balanced. It is all in the mind of the person having the experience as to whether there is some "karma" created, or debt owed.

Why would you not have "perspective" in making this choice? Because of the state of soul growth/awareness that you have at the point of decision. You would not have reached that level of learning. Although others are "working with you" in the decision regarding the "next" life, the decision is yours and they will not move you into perspective you do not have, or are not ready to have.

Do we really choose our parents/ brothers and sisters/ lovers/ spouses and close intimates? Yes. Everything is choice and "contracts" are made between all parties before you come in. There are many "contracts", each being with one other person. "Contracts" are agreements on the parts each will play for the mutual potentials of experience and growth.

Are "contracts" fixed? No. They are the "starting point". They can be changed by choices made through awareness as you go along. They can potentially be changed daily or all totally cancelled, giving you freedom.

If this is the case, then why have I felt so "alien" in my own family? For several potential reasons; primarily because they provide you with a psychological "set up" which predisposes you towards dealing with issues you wish to deal with in this life. Within this context, for instance, each parent will "gift" you with something as you grow. See if you can identify what that might be. Another reason is because the family you chose to come into provided you with a set of genetics that have set you up for the potential for experiencing certain physical attributes.

How can SIDS and other childhood traumatic experiences be explained? In a SIDS situation the soul of the child would agree (contract) with the parents to provide them the experiences derived from the incident. Likewise, for children who die early by any means, including "accidents". The experiences resulting in those remaining behind are the "gift" of the one who passes early. One of the "teachings" may be to learn compassion. One may be to trigger the parents to get heavily involved in the prevention of SIDS or some disease related to the child's death. There are many possible reasons and they are all on purpose, agreed to before they come in and, as mentioned, a gift. There is no telling the total effect any one "gift" may have on those closely or distantly involved.

How can large mass deaths (tsunamis, earthquakes, etc.) be explained? Each individual involved agreed (at a soul level) to experience these events. The reason for each person within the group is most likely not the same. Some may want to experience the event as "something to do" for they know at a level that counts, that they will come back to do something else. Some may die for the benefit of those who survive. Some may die because they want to come back in a different space-time when things will be much different and much "better". It is all choice. You are eternal. Our life is a dream - powerful in its unfolding, but a dream nonetheless. There is one person I know who came back to go down on the Titanic for the drama of it all. Your perspective from the "other side", where you make these choices, is quite different than from this side.

How can incidents such as 9-11 be explained where all those innocent people died? Each of the participants in the 9-11 experience, both on the ground and in the air, chose to take part in the event (at a soul level) because they knew that that event was a pivotal change in the consciousness of the country and the planet. It was the "gift" of their life for a powerful beneficial (to all of humanity) cause. They are to be blessed and thanked, but remember - they still exist. They died in the physical, but not at an energy level, and will come back to experience the wondrous benefits of their contribution. What changed as a result of 9-11? Awareness of the unity of us all, compassion on a very high level, experience of the "uselessness" and "waste" of hate and war, evolvement of the consciousness of the planet, as well as personal and community reasons.

The fact that you may have had your head cut off in the French Revolution, simply because you had money, could well make you swear, on your way to the gallows, that under NO circumstances would you EVER let yourself have money again. The fact that you drowned in one life can make you terrified of water and likewise a falling death can make you terrified of heights. Having been tortured in the Inquisition or marched around a Ziggurat in the Aztec kingdom as you were tortured unto death, can easily affect your attitude towards being hurt and hurting others. All of these experiences eventually come together to allow you to make the decisions on how you wish to express yourself in existence and move you towards your "home", your oneness with the All.

There is an idea that might make sense to you. It is in regards to the concept of heaven, hell and purgatory.

The other side of death is not a "bad" place to be. No matter what one has done in "this" life. There are different levels of vibration, but none are "bad". It is in the reincarnation back into the physical where one experiences hell, purgatory and heaven. And Earth is all of these. The choices made before coming in again are the deciding factors as to what the setup and circumstances will be. The reason for this is that the balancing of the energies need to be experienced in the same context as they were created. The experiencing of appropriate energies allows one to become familiar with opposing energies and, having now been involved in both sides of that energy, make choices as to how one wants to manifest. One can only choose if there is something to choose between. This duality is necessary for growth.

Generally, any single life is not all "bad" or "good", for choices will be possible, yet for those who are in "hell" regardless of circumstances, it can be a pretty terrible place. The presence of heaven and purgatory in one's environment constantly gives one the possibility to see how alternative behavior patterns can be worth pursuing.

There are, of course, degrees. How much "negativity" is in one's life? Is it all terrible? Probably not, but it is a possibility. Here is a real-life experience of what might constitute an "I wonder if I'm in hell" experience:

There was a dream to have a specific car for 25 years and finally it happened. For the person in hell, the car, although supposedly reliable, turned out to have been underwater at some time and had considerable rust. A rear end accident with this car caused the rear axel to break, but in this vibrational environment, the insurance company denied responsibility for the broken rear axel because of the rust. Appeal to the state board also resulted in denial of the claim even though the mechanic who replaced the axel testified that there was no prior damage. And although it wasn't broken before, and there was no indication that it was in any way damaged before, all appeals ended up supporting the insurance company's position. In addition the "car from hell" continued to constantly need repairs and every day something else would seem to pop up. Although the "dream" was achieved, the situational aspect might be a reflection of the "hell" in which the person was living. It is as if one were invited to a banquet and not allowed to have a place at the table.

Change Your Reality

However, the dream still did come true, so the "rest of the vibration" also had its positive aspect in place. It wasn't ALL bad.

This makes an important point which is that this philosophical construct of heaven, purgatory and hell is not "all or nothing". Life is a mix for almost everyone, thus offering opportunities for insights, realizations and choices. These are the mechanisms of potential change and growth. So what happens if one doesn't take an opportunity? Alternate opportunities will come up offering the chance to address the issue again.

One's attitude towards events is an important determining factor as to the nature of where you are vibrationally. It is the emotional reaction that will tell you whether there is an issue to address.

The reasons for a seemingly negative reality can be many. It could be condemnation by others, self-condemnation for "heinous" acts, vows, curses and energies perpetrated by others whom you "wronged". It is possible to determine the sources and change the vibration using the tools and ideas in previous chapters.

It really doesn't matter what the source is. The idea is to get out of "hell" by changing one's vibration. Release (changing one's vibration) will vary with the situation. For many, bringing perspective to the situation by asking forgiveness for yourself and others, and "knowing" emotionally that it was all just experience is sufficient. For others, more specific searches will be necessary.

Remember, there is purpose in everything and for everyone involved. It is well to keep in mind that there are no one way streets in the Universe, for everyone was in any given experience for the purpose of learning and potentially growing. What this means is that whatever happened, it was not totally your fault. It took two to vibrate the situation into reality.

There is one more point to make that is critical in your work to change your vibration. It is that a significant percentage of the events you might consider being "proof" that your life is hell is simply your interpretation and nothing more than the bumps life has to offer. The question is how "bad" and how frequent are the situations.

Along this line, a significant energy causing you to believe that you are in "hell" may be your <u>belief</u> that you are in fact, in hell. Further energizing of this "conclusion" is created when, as a child, you know you are a "bad" person and deserve to be punished. Such energies are carried throughout life unless released through the tools given in previous chapters. There are also potential beliefs accepted during your life indicating that you deserve to be, or "should" be, in hell and thus create the vibration to attract things that support those beliefs.

It is very difficult for a well-intentioned person to forgive themselves for things they did earlier in life. Perspective needs to be brought to these situations to allow that for everyone it was JUST experience. Of course you wouldn't act like that today. That is what growth is about and, yes, change IS possible and indeed, you HAVE changed.

Remember - You live to serve your beliefs.

With all of this seeming negativity, let us not forget the Heaven part. The energies of "Heaven on Earth" that potentially generate lives of joy and balance are all around us. In this book we deal mostly with what can be called the negative pole of duality. The reason for this is primarily to be able to understand it and change our polarity to one of joy, happiness, love and peace. Thereby we attract to ourselves the happier reality we desire and, by birthright, deserve. One of the most important benefits of this perspective is that one can potentially walk in the Peace of understanding that life is Perfection, as it is, for all of us.

Assuming you believe in reincarnation (and by the way there is no "requirement" that you do), one of the reasons there are so many questions is because there are different and unique circumstances that surround every individual. There are many books on the subject, but the most reliable source for your information is you. Ask for information and you can receive it. Try the technique below and be patient with yourself.

I call the technique the "Cocoon" for reasons that will be obvious. It is only one technique. There are many. There is a relatively long introduction to the technique that I think is important to keep perspective.

The Cocoon

The cocoon is a construct of the mind that I shall lead you through to help you create it. Its purpose is to connect you with your Higher Self, Soul energy or however you might perceive the level of consciousness from which you spring. The reason for opening this line of conscious communication is that at that level there is attunement to all of yourself and the cosmic All through your multidimensional DNA. This level also exists outside the space/time continuum in which we experience physical life on this planet. At this level, the true nature of your vibration is available and can be accessed through this methodology. Since there is no time or space at this level, it is the connection to all your other incarnations as well.

There are a couple of VERY important points to be aware of in working with this level of Self.

1. It is you - not someone else. It is an aspect of self you reflect in the greater community of your personality. It is who you are becoming as you expand in awareness.

It is the spirit part of the mind, body and spirit beingness that chose to be in earth at this moment. As you as a child, became you as an adult, this same continuity exists as you in the present expanding to include your own Higher energy. It is an expansion of awareness of who you are. This energy is not some all-knowing judge sitting on a throne and dispensing information and permission. It is YOU. It is very easy to give up your power here on earth to this energy. It will not be allowed for it is not how this place works. Perspective is paramount.

2. You came in to earth to deal with events and circumstances to experience and grow as you chose. You came in to be a conscious individualized creator of your reality. Your soul energy will assist you with answers, but will NOT live your life for you. Not being in the physical, where situations and problems are to be dealt with, it cannot and will not take over your life. YOU must do the work. You are its physical manifestation, it's finger in the pie. Without you and your physicality, there is no finger and there is no pie to experience.

3. Because of the nature of human programming, it is not usually necessary for a Soul energy to become actively involved in the current life. This is because we are set up for automatic responses that will pretty much determine the growth we have chosen. It may seem like we are predestined to certain events and circumstances, but we are not. The correct term is predisposed. In this, we have conscious choice. This is not to say the Soul energy is not present. This level of consciousness is always present, sometimes with greater focus, usually with less. It is much like the nerves in a specific body part. The part is always

there, but generally doesn't get attention by you unless something is out of balance or "requesting assistance".

4. It has been your goal, as part of your Soul level, to establish a strong and more immediate contact. The Soul has been waiting for eons for this because it marks a point of consciousness where one has finally acknowledged that we are more than just a brain in a body. We are part of a much greater Self and the Oneness of the All - It is a very real Knowing that indeed there is a significant non-physical aspect to what we are. You will find that by accepting that your Soul-level energy exists, you have also moved in to an expansion of consciousness that changes drastically the myopic view that is inherent in being in the physical.

5. You are a fragment of your Soul energy. So are all the other lives you have lived. You are how the Soul experiences life in the physical. It cannot experience this venue except through these lives.

6. The Soul is your buddy, not some distant aspect you don't want to bother. It IS interested in becoming a regular part of your consciousness. The littlest point (do I turn left here? are there cops ahead? will this add to the recipe? Thanks for a perfect place to eat and of course, is this for the Highest Good of all concerned?) is worthy of communicating. No item is too small, none too big. All is part of the learning to be the Love that you are. The more you consciously contact it, the more it will participate and the more you will come into harmony with that level of vibration. IF THIS IS YOUR CHOICE!

7. Once established and maintained, a greater focus will be achieved. This is not unlike learning to play an instrument, for the instrument in this case is you.
8. This is only one of many potential communication systems you may establish with your Soul. Many of you already have one or more in place. By intent, the pendulum and the applied kinesiological approach are also valid. So is your intuition and the "first impulse".
9. The cautions concerning discerning whether at some level you are making up "soul" information or really communicating will hold true for ANY system you now have or will establish. Please keep this in consciousness. I give the reasons for the need for discernment and awareness immediately below.

The Huna Science, the spiritual philosophy of the Hawaiian Islands, has as one of its basic tenants that the person is made up of three levels. The Big self, the Middle self and the Little self. The Big self corresponds to the Soul, the Middle self to the consciousness of the present moment and the Little self to the internal musings and goings-on. One of their understandings is that there is no communications directly between the Higher self and the Middle self except through the Little self.

This would say that we can't communicate with our soul energy unless the non-conscious part of us allows it. <u>This is true</u>. And it makes sense. If at a non-conscious level we don't believe it is possible, we aren't worthy, the Soul energy couldn't POSSIBLY be interested, we haven't worked hard enough or any other reason we might harbor, then the communication line is closed. Often to prove we are all these things and more, we will non-consciously make up answers and pretend to be the Soul energy. So you have to constantly test the validity of the responses. How do you do this? By remembering the questions you have asked and their answers. There will be enough right and wrong answers to make this assessment. Test and check all the time, even at the most mundane level. It promotes a stronger and easier communications link. Most of the time it won't make much difference, but sometimes it definitely will. While there may be subjects not allowed by your "little self", and others that are, it is a pretty good guess that if you are making up any answers, all are suspect and the "right" answers are only good guesses.

In the psychic reading and channeling mode, the practitioner sometimes makes up answers from the little-self level because the little self can't deal with being so important or talented and it will make up information constantly. I have known people who have communicated with their higher selves or entities since early childhood who have never doubted their truth, yet it is obvious that the information being shared is not correct and obviously a construct of the little-self/ego.

If this is the case, a potential path to pursue is why am I making up answers? It may well be a rich vein of potential learning. Another potential question is what level of vibrational energy is this information coming from and if not my Soul, then who or what? This latter is certainly possible and is the reason for the cocoon.

The basic idea behind the cocoon is to provide a safe haven for you to communicate. By its very nature it keeps out unwanted vibrations of lower frequency.

The first step is to find a place where you can be totally relaxed and undisturbed for a period of time (minimum an hour, probably a bit longer, depending on you and your level of intensity, curiosity and drive). Next is to provide an atmosphere for contemplation. This may be low light, soft music (or not) and a general feeling of harmony and safety. You might want to provide something to take notes with close by. <u>Perhaps a voice-activated recorder.</u>

Position is not important, although I have found that being on my own bed is most conducive to relaxing because it is safe and where I sleep. After some practice, the cocoon can be created in any environment in an instant. This simply takes becoming comfortable with the concept and use of the tool. In fact once in it, you may choose to recreate it often and "travel" in it during your daily routines. The options are endless and totally dependent on you.

What happens in the cocoon is different for every person. Information will lead you to questions that will lead to other information. Limitations may become obvious in which case that leads to another path. Consider it a joyful adventure in the safety of your own place. There are no "correct" answers or path. As in life, this is just an experience. Your attitude and programming will have a considerable effect on what happens.

There is no one to judge you except yourself and here this must be suspended. It makes no difference where the information you get is coming from, only that you are opening up your mind to the possibility of a different paradigm. Do not let your mind take over. It will tend to question everything - "Where did THAT come from?" - "What does that mean?" - "I must be making this up."

SO WHAT!!

These are all mascinations of the mind, and this is an HEART trip. Wait until you are completely finished and then journal or assess what happened. Most of all, approach it as fun. You are a manifestation of a joyful soul experiencing life in its fullness. Lighten up. Let go and let Joy. Save the serious stuff for another session. This is simply for acquaintance purposes.

So let's go.

If you are doing this from the book, you will have to prop your self up and read a step and then do it. Although it is easier with someone guiding you on this first journey, this will work very well if you remain patient with yourself. Remember there is no hurry and no requirements to perform in any manner. First read each step and then do it. Keep joyful and calm - as I said, this can be fun.

If, for some reason, you find yourself extremely anxious, try some self-talk about being safe, exploring a new adventure and such. If your anxiety continues at uncomfortable levels, then you need to go to the "tools" in Chapter 4 and find out why.

1. Close your eyes for a moment and imagine a small pyramid of white light in your heart. Everyone has one, for this is the communication device between you and your "Soul". Just focus on it for a little while, notice its intensity, its light and feel the wonderfulness of its beingness. Do the best you can - that is good enough. Then open your eyes, remembering the pyramid and read the next step. Please be patient and take time. This attitude will materially assist in the journey.
2. Close your eyes again, refocusing on the pyramid and allow that the light from it is beginning to expand to fill your heart. Sense the warmth of it and just watch it progress. Allow this light to flow outside your heart and fill your chest. Again feel the warmth as the whole adventure unfolds. Once there, allow it to continue to expand at whatever rate you feel is comfortable to move up your neck, down your arms, down your torso and into your legs, into your head, hands and feet and stop it at the edge of your body. Get as comfortable with this visualization as you can and stay with it for as long as it feels "right". See if you can come to sense its warmth as it permeates every cell, organ and tissue

of your body. Allow, simply as part of what is going on, that it is bringing balance, synergy and healing to your entire body and will continue to do so while you continue your progress. Open your eyes only when you feel it is just the right time, keeping in tact as part of your consciousness, what you have just done.

3. Sit for a moment with your eyes open totally aware of your surroundings and still conscious of the internal light that fills your body. Know that this is the light of your Soul energy and has created a vibrational protection within you that will keep negative energy away. Feel the safety and comfort of the creation. When ready again, close your eyes and refocus on the light shimmering at the edge of your body. Now allow it to expand outside your body just enough to create a cocoon in which you exist. This is the safety cocoon in which you will expand your beingness to the point of allowing communications with your Higher Self/Soul. Be with it for a bit and when ready, again open your eyes.

4. Totally conscious of your surroundings, again be conscious of the cocoon in which you now find yourself. KNOW that you are safe. The healing continues automatically while you visualize yourself just sitting in comfort and being totally relaxed. You can "wear" this cocoon at any time for any reason. I will share with you how to create it instantaneously at the end of the session. For now simply know that it is available to you at any time. When you are ready, close your eyes again, keeping in mind that you are in a cocoon of light that is of the vibrational frequency of your Higher Self/Soul. Ask that your Soul energy join you in a manner that you can recognize. There can be any one of many ways it will choose to be present. It

may be visual, it may be a feeling, it may be a sound, or a voice. It is up to your Higher Self/Soul how It will manifest and it will be tuned specifically to who you are at this moment. Stay with the manifestation for a bit and become comfortable with it. When it feels comfortable, again open your eyes. If you have trouble discerning any change, you may be trying too hard, for the vibrational change, of necessity is a finer one, and the fear of not performing, or it not happening or whatever will override it. If after a reasonable time you still can't manifest any change, open your eyes, remaining in the cocoon.

For those of you for whom this did not work, know this: Your soul energy full well knows that you are working at communicating. The request you have made is in place and will be addressed at a time that will work for you. This can be at bedtime, or walking somewhere, just sitting, or going through the steps again. That you wish it to be true, it WILL manifest - for your soul energy is as desirous of it happening as you. Be patient and simply know that at a perfect time something will "click" and you will achieve the awareness of Its Presence. At that point come back to a comfortable place, put yourself in the cocoon and take the next step. For now remain in the cocoon if you would like, and go about the rest of your day. At a time like this, patience is well nigh impossible. You will have to exercise your will in this matter. Go forth in the joy of knowing you have taken the first step. It WILL happen. Guaranteed.

For those of you who have had a response, continue. Or you may want to just sit and be present to yourself for a while. There IS no hurry. Seek harmony and ease in the journey.

5. Tell yourself that whatever happens you will remember everything. See if you can retain the

feeling of Its presence in a waking state. Notice how you feel with this "additional" level of consciousness awakened within you. Sit for a while and when ready, again close your eyes. Still fully in the cocoon, reaffirm the presence of your Higher Self/Soul. If this has faded a bit, ask it to come back into consciousness to a level that you can again recognize. Say "hi", "thanks for coming", "welcome to my life", and ask if there is anything it would like to share with you. This might be anything; a thought, words, a picture, a feeling - literally anything. Make note in waking consciousness what has happened. Open your eyes keeping the contact in place and read number six.

6. Again close your eyes and ask your Higher Self/Soul to bring you a message that might be of value to you at this time. Again it can be anything but note its nature and content. If you don't understand what you've gotten, ask for clarification and be patient while it works with you on this new information system. It takes time to establish new patterns. At this point again open your eyes and make a note of what was shared and your interpretation. Remain in the cocoon and in consciousness with your Higher Self/Soul.

If this has been comfortable and productive to you, then we are ready to move into the use of this system to deal with limiting programming. However, I would suggest taking a little time off to let the new paradigm seep into your hologram before continuing. Perhaps an evening or a day. It will make a difference in the flow. During this "rest" time put your awareness back on the cocoon as often as it comes to mind. Each time re-feel the comfort and safety of this new device and think on the wonder of it all.

Here I would like to share with you the instantaneous method of creating the cocoon and a communication medium for you and your Higher Self/Soul.

The cocoon provides protection from negativity just in its creation. Many keep this around them much of the time. It must be checked in on often enough to see if it is still up and running. If not, do the instantaneous jump-start again. It is this:

As you breathe in, think the capital letter "I", followed by the capitalized word "AM". At the same time put your consciousness on the pyramid in your heart. At full breath, release the breath comfortably while thinking in capitalized letters "LOVE". As this occurs picture the light from the pyramid instantaneously flowing out and creating the cocoon. At the finish of the out breath, the cocoon is fully operational. You can do it anywhere and anytime you choose for whatever purpose you feel is appropriate. When you do this, however, you are also tuning into your own higher vibrational energies. This is a good thing. It confirms your higher intentions of being.

7. Back in a comfortable place, create the cocoon again by either going through the steps or using the method shared above and call in your Higher Self/Soul. Even if you aren't particularly aware of the presence of your soul energy, ask once again if there is anything it would like to share with you. Wait to see if there is and remember what it might be and your interpretation. There is another capability the soul has in relation to communicating with you. You may have already experienced it when asking it for a message. It is the "light pictograph" explained in Chapter 4.

Any picture you get from your soul energy is this "light pictograph". The message contains a great deal of information all at once. As mentioned before, it can be thought of as a packet that contains everything pertinent to the answer shared.

Now to looking into other lives. First state your intent, which is to look into other lives. Thank your soul energy for assisting you in this matter.

It should be noted that everyone is unique and there are no "standard" responses.

Again find yourself in a comfortable place and put yourself in the cocoon. Sit with it for a moment and ask your soul energy to come forth. Assuming you feel this has happened, ask it for a picture of the life that is most pertinent to this one. Be patient. When a picture forms, and it may be just a wisp flying through your consciousness - "catch" it and don't question it. Once you have it, then begin to ask questions.

The questions will have to be unique to your experience. You will have to make them up from you imagination. The ones I share now are just an example.

It should also be noted that the soul energy, having just gotten this opportunity to be with you in consciousness, may have a slightly different agenda and a picture which is not representative of another life may come up. Whatever it is, ask what is it the soul energy would like to share about this picture. How does it relate to this life? Be persistent until you get answers that make sense to you. Don't be afraid to say you don't understand and need further clarification.

Let's say that you do get pictures. You can ask questions about them such as:

> Where am I in this picture?
> What is it you would like to share about this?

And when you're finished;
Is there anything else you would like to share with me about this life or picture?

When working with other lives, there may be subjects which you would like to pursue, such as:

What was my happiest life?

Did I know someone (father, mother, friend, lover, acquaintance etc.) in another life? When was that?

Did I live in some city?

Play an instrument?

Have families?

Why am I afraid of water? burning? falling? etc.

The questions are endless and only limited by your curiosity.

When looking into another life, you can fast forward it to another time to find out how it worked out. Look around and see if you can determine a time and place where this is going on. Did I have family? Do I know them in this life? And, when you think you are finished, ask if there is anything else your soul energy would like to share with you concerning this life. Then, if there is something, get that and ask again if there is anything else, and then, are we ready to move on to another life.

You will find that you will indeed remember the information shared and be able to recall it with clarity. There also may be "fallout" from some experience in this modality. The "fallout" could be additional understandings that can come any time when you are thinking of the experience and may be "Oh - that's why I do this, or am afraid of something."

As was said before, these adventures in consciousness can be either curiosities or of some assistance in becoming free of limiting programming. The journey is yours to explore.

There is an analogy that might be of interest concerning the learning sequence on this planet:

We start off in Dark School. Here are what might be called "negative" expressions that give us experience to see what it is like to be dark. We also experience many alternatives (dark and light) during this period to again give us an experiential choice as to how we might like to manifest as we continue our growth. At some point we make a decision that we prefer to express ourselves in a "positive" way. At this point we graduate "Dark School" and enter "Light School. Here we are exposed to "light concepts" and the nature of our Universal beingness.

Being humans, we want what we want and we want it now, and naturally want all of the benefits and capabilities of "light work" NOW. What we tend to miss is that "Light School" has many learnings to be experienced and many "classes" to attend. There is "Light 101, 102, 201, 202, etc.

In this context, we have as our basis for experience "Dark School", and make our actions and decisions from this base, so there is much to change and learn. Reprogramming of "old "energies and behavior patterns is a natural process of attending "Light School". There is much residual that needs to be addressed.

Graduation from "Light School" occurs when the concept of the Perfection of "what is" is accepted and the concepts of "light and dark", "right and wrong", "good and bad" and other duality ideas meld into the Knowing that there is nothing that is not of the Universal Oneness and the seeming darkness and lightness are equally required for the expansion of the Consciousness of the Universe. It is the point at which there remains no judgment about anything. All is recognized as integral and necessary for the unfoldment of Consciousness.

The physical representative of this is the Yin and Yang circle, wherein each side has a dot of the other in the middle to symbolize the presence of both in making the Whole. As mentioned before, some say that the last judgment is the last time we judge ourselves.

This "graduation" brings us into harmony with the Universal All and is the "home" we all seek.

This is not a kindergarten,

Change Your Reality

It is a graduate school.

Many wonder if after "graduation" we leave the planet. The answer is: it is choice. Many stay to "walk between two worlds" and assist others who are on their path of becoming.

Home is where the heart is.

We are all going to graduate, so enjoy the journey as you progress, and keep the perspective that it is all Perfect in its unfoldment.

There may be some hidden requirements that you have set up for yourself by which you measure and judge yourself in regards to your "readiness" to move forward. Here are some examples that you might check to see if they apply to you:

Not good enough - This is really "not God enough". We tend to think that only light is on the path to enlightenment and any "dark" thoughts, actions or experiences automatically preclude our "acceptance" for "graduation". This comes from the ignorance of not knowing that there is nothing that is not of God and that darkness and light are only two halves of the whole. The Yin and Yang is the essence of the acceptance of everything going to make up the whole. Remember, the white side has a dot of dark, and the dark, a spot of white. It is essential to remember and accept this as your "truth". You are a Perfect reflection of the Universal Oneness.

>AS YOU ARE,
>RIGHT NOW.

Judgment - You have judged yourself as "unworthy"(and all the similar detrimental expressions) forever. You have required a performance of yourself that has generally been beyond your capability to achieve and therefore judged yourself as a "failure". Nothing could be farther from the truth. Success and failure are an illusion we have come to think of as "truth".

It is all just experience in order to allow you to choose how you want to express yourself in the physical, and asses whether you want to change. In order to make a choice you have to have contrary experiences from which to choose. This is easy to see, but difficult to accept within your own psyche.

It is worth noting here that the circumstances provided in this world will not change. What will change, as you develop, is your attitude towards them - resulting eventually in being "transparent" to negativity.

Once you have moved to the place of accepting the Perfection of who, what, where, how and why you are now, you will find the harmony of your life to be peaceful and beautiful, regardless of the circumstances you are experiencing. This is possible for everyone. Yes it takes work, and perhaps a bit of obsessive/compulsive behavior, but it does not render you dysfunctional. Quite to the contrary, it renders you a magnificent and conscious part of that which we call the Universe.

Chapter 10

FROM omnipotence
TO OMNIPOTENCE

When we are first born, and for some time into life, the child believes and acts as if it is omnipotent: all-powerful. It is mother and the universe and everything it can interrelate with at every level. It doesn't take too long, though, before "reality" sets in and the child learns it really doesn't have much power to do anything except cry. As the rest of life proceeds, we tend to feel less and less powerful and more and more the victims of the world around us. If not the victims, then at least not able to control much of our internal world. This includes not only our health and our automatic responses to much of what goes on, but certainly our external world where it all seems out of our control.

As time passes we may become aware that we do have a say to some extent and are not powerless, however, the feeling of not having much power tends to persist, that is until we move into awareness. Eventually this leads to the understanding that indeed we might, and then indeed we do create our reality 100%. When this happens we realize that in our reality we are in fact Omnipotent. Is this real?

The answer is yes. How can we know this?

How do we know anything? Through experience. How do we come to believe what was once considered "impossible"? Through experience. What kind of experience? It is obviously very individualized, but in general there are actual personal physical experiences. You thought about something and it happened, you wanted something and it appeared. You wanted to create something and it was done.

As you become aware of your thoughts having created something and this happens more often, the idea of you actually causing whatever it was becomes more of a possibility. Somewhere in here the idea of being able to totally create your reality begins to look more likely. That's how.

As mentioned before, according to the Kryon material, (www. KRYON.com) we do indeed have the capability in this "new" energy to live 900 years, the lifespan for which the body was actually "designed". The magnetic and crystalline grids have been changed and our DNA is really a multidimensional 12 layer roadmap to our ascension into higher vibrational capabilities while we are here on earth so we can "walk" in both worlds.

In this book we talk about creating anything you want to Be, Do or Have as your God-given birthright. Well what now? What are you going to do with all this information? Assuming you believe it and it may take some time (because we are in the physical) how is this going to change your life?

First, if you are relatively normal, you need evidence of this that can move you from almost knowing to Knowing. Once this is available and has become part of your paradigm, what are you going to do?

The answer is simple. Whatever you want. Maybe you'll have to decide at some point. One thing about living such a long period is that the urgency to getting anything done is gone. You can still plant a black walnut tree orchard and harvest the veneer logs in 75 years and still have lots of time to spend the money... Or what else?

A friend of mine says that if he had infinite power he would do nothing because he also would realize that everything was perfect just as it is. Everyone on the planet chose to come here and is doing what they have already chosen to do, so what is there to do, except make himself happy. And what would that take? Whatever it takes, for him or for you.

Yet another friend suggests that the goal of ceremony is to eventually walk in ceremony, thus needing no ceremony, just being.

Yet for others, there is a driving desire to serve and help others on their path. They know that "like vibrations attract" will bring to them whomever is ready to hear what they have to share. It is all choice.

Now - why all this? Just to make you think.

A couple of stories before we close:

Long ago and far away there was a planet that was inhabited by people much like us. This planet had developed a society that was much like ours in that most people were extraordinarily selfish and considered their own interests above others. They were short sighted about the effects their society had on the planet and others, and in general could be considered "baby" or "young" soul fragments.

There were, of course a number of "mature" and "old" souls on the planet, but they were in the vast minority and could not affect an increase in consciousness. At one point one of these very "old" souls decided that the society, indeed the entire planet wasn't worth continuing, and, through his mind, destroyed the entire planet and its population. Several billion people died along with the planetary consciousness in the resulting cataclysm.

At some point the individual decided that although he knew there was nothing "wrong" with doing this because consciousness is forever, that this was not the way he wanted to express himself. He decided that he needed some additional experience. So he came to earth to once again experience the self-centeredness of a population, only this time to get the perspective that everything is Perfect as it is and everyone is experiencing what they need to, to progress on their cosmic path. He got it, and the story is true.

What does this say? If you believe it, we are indeed infinitely powerful, and our growth is towards how we find our own expression acceptable. Doesn't matter what you do; the Universe will continue regardless, as will its growth in consciousness, and yours.

Does this say that someone with that kind of power is going to destroy us? No. Not this time. The reason is that there is a very powerful movement, although almost invisible in the media, that is working for us to make it this time. There are many "old" souls on the planet and more coming in all the time. There is more than hope, this is a certainty. You may want to stick around and help make it happen.

And one more: It is my story and it has a point to ponder. I contracted rheumatic fever when I was 18 months old and as a result was not allowed to participate in group activities throughout grade school and much of high school. As a result of this I was constantly rejected by my fellow students, as kids are wont to do.

To counter this, and fulfill one of the basic human needs, which is to belong in order to be safe, I developed a capability to understand how people worked and what was necessary to make me feel safe. This continued throughout the school years until I was pretty good at being able to use and manipulate people in order to make myself feel safe. Of course this was less than successful, so the work continued. By the end of college I was quite capable at it and was "accepted" for the most part by others, but internally it was a quest that was incapable of being fulfilled.

I thought I was doing well until I had a reading from a woman who told me about some danger one of my brothers was in on a specific day in a specific way in the future. She was correct and it lead to many questions about how she could know the future and eventually to how could I use and manipulate such a capability into keeping myself safe.

Thus began a journey of exploration into the esoteric. Many years later I was still at it but had, in my conscious mind, let go of the "use and manipulate" reasoning and proceeded down a spiritual path. One day, in pursuing why I was not getting "right" answers, I came to find out that I was still operating at a deep level trying to use and manipulate the Universe in order to keep myself safe.

Well, the jigger was up. Knowing that the Universe is not a fool and can't be "used and manipulated" I found myself in a quandary. I had professed that what I wanted to do what was for the highest good, but came to realize that just maybe it might mean giving up my dreams. Dreams of collecting cars, traveling and whatever. Maybe the Universe would want me somewhere else and the "dreams" would have to be let go.

I knew what the ultimate outcome would be, but could not bring myself to make the final decision. I was in a confused place for quite a long time. How sincere was I really about surrendering to the Universal Oneness? Even though I knew that the Universe doesn't care and everything is Perfect as it is, I still held the deep-seated belief that what I wanted just may not be what the Universe "wanted" for me. To me, surrender meant giving up my personal agenda.

One morning I was sitting in bed and again thinking on this when I heard a familiar voice, as I had heard for many years. It was my own. No different than talking to myself over a lifetime. But this time something was different. It was the energy around the situation. It was so powerfully full of love that I immediately began to cry. It was impossible to maintain any semblance of normalcy. The energy was extremely intense. While not being able to think clearly, the voice was as calm and loving as I could imagine and it asked:

"Would you do something for me?"

There was only one possible answer in this energy and I burbled "yes, of course - anything."
The voice continued, so clearly, so gently,

> "Pursue your dreams.
> For your dreams
> Are My dreams for you".

I leave you with this:

> Pursue your dreams,
> For the Universe's dreams are
> It's dreams for you.

thanks

www.ingramcontent.com/pod-product-compliance
Ingram Content Group UK Ltd.
Pitfield, Milton Keynes, MK11 3LW, UK
UKHW041951230426
12048UKWH00008B/264